Library
Knowledge
Royal Cornw... ...ral health

Third Edition

Edited by

Michael Edgar
Emeritus Professor of Dental Science,
The University of Liverpool, UK

Colin Dawes
Professor, Department of Oral Biology, Faculty of Dentistry,
University of Manitoba, Winnipeg MB, Canada

Denis O'Mullane
Emeritus Professor/Consultant, Oral Health Services Research Centre,
University Dental School and Hospital, Wilton, Cork, Ireland

2004

Published by the British Dental Association
64 Wimpole Street, London, W1G 8YS

Contributors

Susan M. Higham
Professor of Oral Biology
Department of Clinical Dental Sciences
School of Dentistry
Liverpool, UK

Jacob M. ('Bob') ten Cate
Professor of Experimental Preventive Dentistry
and Director of Research, Academic Centre for
Dentistry Amsterdam (ACTA), The Netherlands
Director, Netherlands Institute for Dental Sciences

Jonathan A. Ship
Professor, Department of Oral Medicine; NYU
College of Dentistry
Professor, Department of Medicine; NYU School
of Medicine
New York, USA

Peter M Smith
Senior Lecturer in Oral Biology
Department of Clinical Dental Sciences
School of Dentistry
Liverpool, UK

Jorma Tenovuo
Professor and Chairman of Cariology
Institute of Dentistry
University of Turku, Finland

Helen Whelton
Director, Oral Health Services Research Centre
Senior Lecturer in Dental Public Health and
Preventive Dentistry
University Dental School and Hospital
Wilton
Cork, Ireland

Preface

This third edition of *Saliva and Oral Health* has been made necessary by the continuing success of the previous edition; with continuing demand and no further copies available, rather than merely order a reprint the opportunity was seized to update and improve upon both the text and the figures.

As occurred when the previous edition was written, there have been changes in the authorship of this new version. The chapters on *Salivary influences on the oral microflora* by Professor Bill Bowen, and on *The functions of salivary proteins* by Professors Don Hay and Bill Bowen, have been combined into a single chapter entitled *Protective functions of saliva* by Professor Jorma Tenovuo, whose expertise and flair has been most welcome. The chapter on *Xerostomia: diagnosis, management and clinical complications*, formerly by Professor Leo Sreebny, has been rewritten by Professor Jonathon Ship under the modified title *Xerostomia: aetiology, diagnosis, management and clinical implications*. All other authors remain the same as in the previous edition, and all have taken the opportunity of adding new material and (to a lesser extent) removing information now seen as of less importance to the intended reader. Professor Colin Dawes, previously the author of two chapters, has now in addition shared the editorship with the two former editors of the book.

The book is still aimed principally at 'the progressive and inquisitive practitioner', but we have learnt from feedback that not only undergraduate and postgraduate dental students, but also other health professionals, have found it useful. We believe that we can detect a change in the attitude of dentists, and also of medical colleagues, in recognizing the importance of saliva in the maintenance of oral health, and hope that this little book has in some degree contributed to this change.

In preparing the new material the authors have been greatly helped by the work of previous contributors, who are listed below. The authors and editors met prior to the IADR General Session in Gothenburg in June 2003 to discuss the chapter outlines, and submitted the manuscripts to the editors by September. The edited chapters and figures were submitted to the publishers in October. We are very grateful for the cooperation of all involved in the rapid production of the new edition. We are also greatly indebted to the Wm Wrigley Jr Co, in the persons first of Niels Hoegh-Guldberg and then Dr Michael Dodds, for funding the meeting of authors in Gothenburg and for underwriting the costs of the publication.

Michael Edgar
Colin Dawes
Denis O'Mullane

Contents

First edition 1990
Second edition 1996
Third edition 2004

ISBN 0 904588 74 2

Printed and bound by
Dennis Barber Limited,
Lowestoft, Suffolk

Introduction: the anatomy and physiology of salivary glands

Helen Whelton

Saliva is the glandular secretion that constantly bathes the teeth and the oral mucosa. It is constituted by the secretions of the three, paired major salivary glands, the parotid, submandibular and sublingual, the minor salivary glands and the gingival fluid.

The presence of saliva is vital to the maintenance of healthy oral tissues. Severe reduction of salivary output not only results in a rapid deterioration in oral health but also has a detrimental impact on quality of life for the sufferer. Patients suffering from dry mouth experience difficulty with eating, swallowing, speech, retention of dentures, taste alteration, oral hygiene, trauma and ulceration of the oral mucosa, a burning sensation of the mucosa, oral infections including *Candida* and rapidly progressive dental caries. Dry mouth or xerostomia is becoming increasingly common in developed countries where adults are living longer. Polypharmacy is very common among the older adult population and many of the commonly prescribed drugs cause a reduction in salivary flow. Xerostomia also occurs in Sjögren's syndrome, which is not an uncommon condition. In addition to specific diseases of the salivary glands, salivary flow is usually severely impaired following radiotherapy in the head and neck area for cancer treatment in both children and adults of all ages. Clearly, xerostomia is a problem that faces an increasingly large proportion of the population. An understanding of saliva and its role in oral health will help to promote awareness among health care workers of the problem, its prevention and treatment.

There is an extensive body of research on saliva as a diagnostic fluid. It has been used to indicate caries susceptibility; it has also been used to reflect systemic physiological and pathological changes that are mirrored in saliva. Saliva is easily available for non-invasive collection and analysis. It can be used to monitor the presence and level of hormones, drugs, antibodies, micro-organisms and ions.

This chapter will provide an overview of the functions of saliva, the anatomy and histology of salivary glands, the physiology of saliva formation, the constituents of saliva and the use of saliva as a diagnostic fluid, including its role in caries risk assessment. Much of the material in this chapter will be covered in more detail in later chapters.

Functions of saliva

The complexity of this oral fluid is perhaps best appreciated by the consideration of its many and varied functions. The functions of saliva are largely protective; however, it also has other functions. Table 1.1 provides an overview of many of these functions. More detail is provided in subsequent chapters as indicated.

The changes in plaque pH following ingestion of various foodstuffs are illustrated in Figure 1.1. The graph is referred to as a Stephan Curve after the scientist who first described it in about 1940 when he measured changes in plaque pH using antimony probe micro-electrodes.

As can be seen in Figure 1.1 the resting plaque pH is approximately 6.7. Following a sucrose rinse the plaque pH is reduced to less than 5.0 within a few minutes. Demineralization of the enamel takes place below the critical pH of about 5.5. Plaque pH stays below the critical pH for approximately 15–20 minutes and does not return to normal until about 40 minutes after the ingestion of the sucrose rinse. Once plaque pH recovers to a level above the critical pH, the enamel is remineralized in the presence of saliva and oral fluids, which are supersaturated with respect to hydroxyapatite and fluorapatite. The shape of the Stephan curve varies among individuals and the rate of recovery of the plaque pH is largely determined by the buffering capacity and urea content of saliva and the velocity of the salivary film (*see* Chapters 5 and 6). The buffering capacity of saliva increases with increasing flow rates as the bicarbonate ion concentration increases. The carbonic acid/bicarbonate system is the major buffer in stimulated saliva.

$$\text{H}^+ + \text{HCO}_3^- \xrightarrow{\hspace{0.5cm}} \overset{\text{carbonic anhydrase}}{\text{H}_2\text{CO}_3 \rightarrow \text{H}_2\text{O} + \text{CO}_2}$$

Hydronium and bicarbonate ions form carbonic acid which forms carbon dioxide and water.

Table 1.1 Functions of saliva

Fluid/Lubricant	Coats mucosa and helps to protect against mechanical, thermal and chemical irritation. Assists smooth air flow, speech and swallowing.
Ion reservoir	Solution supersaturated with respect to tooth mineral facilitates remineralization of the teeth. Statherin and acidic proline-rich proteins in saliva inhibit spontaneous precipitation of calcium phosphate salts (see Chapter 8).
Buffer	Helps to neutralize plaque pH after eating, thus reducing time for demineralization (see Chapter 6).
Cleansing	Clears food and aids swallowing (see Chapter 5).
Antimicrobial actions	Specific (eg sIgA) and non-specific (eg lysozyme, lactoferrin and myeloperoxidase) antimicrobial mechanisms help to control the oral microflora (see Chapter 7).
Agglutination	Agglutinins in saliva aggregate bacteria resulting in accelerated clearance of bacterial cells (see Chapter 7). Examples are mucins and parotid saliva glycoproteins.
Pellicle formation	Thin (1–10 µm) protective diffusion barrier formed on enamel from salivary proteins.
Digestion	The enzyme α-amylase is the most abundant salivary enzyme; it splits starchy foods into maltose, maltotriose and dextrins (see Chapter 7).
Taste	Saliva acts as a solvent thus allowing interaction of foodstuff with taste buds to facilitate taste (see Chapter 3).
Excretion	As the oral cavity is technically outside the body, substances that are secreted in saliva are excreted. This is a very inefficient excretory pathway as reabsorption may occur further down the intestinal tract.
Water balance	Under conditions of dehydration, salivary flow is reduced, dryness of the mouth and information from osmoreceptors are translated into decreased urine production and increased drinking (integrated by the hypothalamus, see Chapter 4).

Anatomy and histology

The type of salivary secretion varies according to gland. Secretions from the parotid gland are serous or watery in consistency, those from the submandibular and sublingual glands, and particularly the minor mucous glands, are much more viscous due to their glycoprotein content. The histology of the gland therefore varies according to gland type.

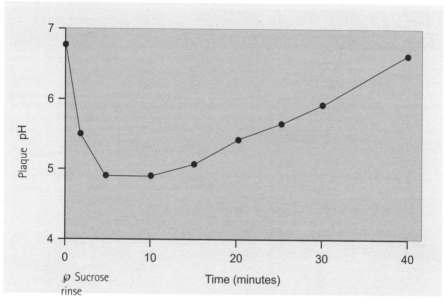

Fig. 1.1 Stephan Curve illustrating the changes in plaque pH over time following a sucrose rinse

All of the salivary glands develop in a similar way. An ingrowth of epithelium from the stomatodeum extends deeply into the ectomesenchyme and branches profusely to form all the working parts of the gland. The surrounding ectomesenchyme then differentiates to form the connective tissue component of the gland, ie the capsule and fibrous septa that divide the gland into lobes. These developments take place between four and 12 weeks of embryonic life, the parotids being the first to develop and the sublingual and minor salivary glands being the last. Figure 1.2 shows some of the relations of the parotid and the submandibular and sublingual glands.

The parotids are the largest salivary glands. They are wedge-shaped with the base of the wedge lying superficially covered by fascia and the parotid capsule. They are situated in front of the ear and behind the ramus of the mandible. The apex of the wedge is the deepest part of the gland. The gland is intimately associated with the peripheral branches of the facial nerve (CN VII). This relationship is particularly noticeable when an inferior alveolar nerve block is inadvertently administered too high up in a child. In this situation the anaesthetic is delivered into the parotid gland and the facial nerve is

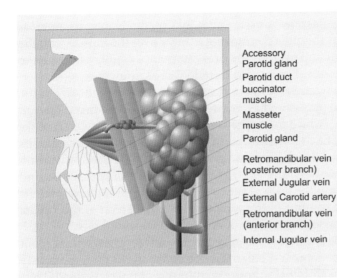

Fig. 1.2 Anatomy of the salivary glands

Accessory
Parotid gland

Parotid duct
buccinator
muscle

Masseter
muscle

Parotid gland

Retromandibular vein
(posterior branch)

External Jugular vein

External Carotid artery

Retromandibular vein
(anterior branch)

Internal Jugular vein

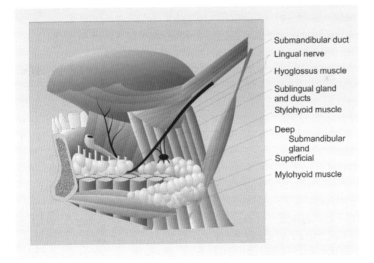

Submandibular duct

Lingual nerve

Hyoglossus muscle

Sublingual gland
and ducts

Stylohyoid muscle

Deep
    Submandibular
    gland
Superficial

Mylohyoid muscle

anaesthetized, thus resulting in an alarming appearance of a drooping eyelid, which is of course temporary.

The parotid duct is thick walled, formed by the union of the ductules, which drain the lobules of the glands. It emerges at the anterior border of the gland on the surface of the masseter muscle and hooks medially over its anterior border. It can be felt at this point by moving a finger over the muscle with the jaw clenched. The duct opens into the oral cavity in a papilla opposite the second upper molar tooth. The parotid secretions are serous.

The submandibular gland is variable in size being about half the size of the parotid. Its superficial part is wedged between the body of the mandible and the mylohyoid muscle (which forms the floor of the mouth). The gland hooks around the sharply defined posterior border of the mylohyoid muscle and its smaller, deep part lies above the mylohyoid in the floor of the mouth. The thin walled duct runs forward in the angle between the side of the tongue and mylohyoid. It opens into the floor of the mouth underneath the anterior part of the tongue, on the summit of the sublingual papilla lateral to the lingual fraenum. The secretions are a mixture of mucous and serous fluids.

The sublingual is the smallest of the paired major salivary glands being about one-fifth the size of the submandibular. It is situated in the floor of the mouth beneath the sublingual folds of mucous membrane. Numerous small ducts (8–20) open into the mouth on the summit of the sublingual fold. It is predominantly a mucous gland.

Minor salivary glands are situated on the lateral border of the tongue, the posterior part of the palate and in the buccal and labial mucosa. They are small mucosal glands with primarily a mucous secretion.

Structure of salivary glands

The working parts of the salivary glandular tissue (Fig. 1.3) consist of the secretory end pieces (acini) and the branched ductal system. In serous glands (eg the parotids), the cells in the end piece are arranged in a roughly spherical form. In mucous glands they tend to be arranged in a tubular configuration with a larger central lumen. In both types of gland the cells in the end piece surround a lumen and this is the start of the ductal system. There are three types of duct present in all salivary glands. The fluid first passes through the intercalated ducts which have low cuboidal epithelium and a narrow lumen. From there the secretions enter the striated ducts which are lined by more columnar cells with many mitochondria. Finally, the saliva passes through the excretory ducts where the cell type is cuboidal until the terminal part which is lined with stratified squamous epithelium.

End pieces may contain mucous cells, serous cells or a mixture of both. A salivary gland can consist of a varied mixture of these types of end pieces. In

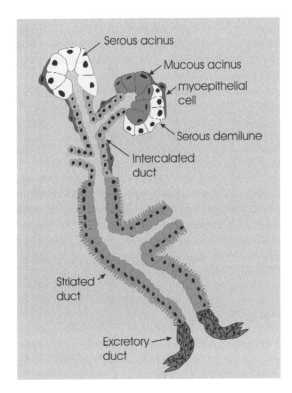

Fig. 1.3 Structure of the salivary glands

mixed glands, the mucous acini are capped by a serous demilune. In addition, myoepithelial cells surround the end piece, their function being to assist in propelling the secretion into the ductal system. The gland and its specialized nerve and blood supply are supported by a connective tissue stroma.

Formation of saliva

The fluid formation in salivary glands occurs in the end pieces (acini) where serous cells produce a watery seromucous secretion and mucous cells produce a viscous mucin-rich secretion. These secretions arise by the formation of interstitial fluid from blood in capillaries, which is then modified by the end piece cells. This modified interstitial fluid is secreted into the lumen. From the lumen it passes through the ductal system where it is further modified. Most of the modification occurs in the striated ducts where ion exchange takes place and the secretion is changed from an isotonic solution to a hypotonic one. The composition of saliva is further modified in the excretory ducts before it is finally secreted into the mouth (*see* Chapter 2 for a detailed account of saliva secretory mechanisms).

Nerve supply

The glands receive both parasympathetic and sympathetic nerve supplies. Secretion is controlled mainly by parasympathetic impulses from the salivary nuclei. These are located approximately at the juncture of the pons and the medulla and are excited by both taste and mechanical stimuli from the tongue and other areas of the mouth via afferent sensory fibres. Salivation can also be stimulated or inhibited by impulses arriving in the salivary nuclei from higher centres of the central nervous system. For example, in stressful situations dry mouth sometimes occurs, not as a result of any direct sympathetic inhibition as was previously thought, but rather as a result of the inhibitory effect of higher centres on salivary nuclei.

Reflexes originating in the stomach and upper intestines also stimulate salivation; for example, when very irritating foods are swallowed or when a person is nauseated the saliva serves to dilute or neutralize the irritating substances.

Sympathetic stimulation can also increase salivary flow to a moderate extent but much less so than parasympathetic stimulation. Sympathetic impulses are more likely to influence salivary composition by increasing exocytosis from certain cells. The sympathetic nerves originate in the spinal cord, synapse in the superior cervical ganglia and then travel along the blood vessels to the salivary glands. Salivary composition may also be influenced by hormones such as androgens, oestrogens, glucocorticoids and peptide hormones.

Blood supply

The blood supply to the glands also influences secretion. An extensive blood supply is required for the rapid secretion of saliva. There is a concentration of capillaries around the striated ducts where ionic exchange takes place whilst a lesser density supplies the terminal secretory acini. The process of salivation indirectly dilates the blood vessels thus providing increased nutrition as needed. Salivary secretion is usually accompanied by a large increase in blood flow to the glands.

Physiology

Composition
The composition of saliva varies according to many factors including the gland type from which it is secreted. The average composition of a sample of whole saliva is shown in Table 1.2.

Flow rate
Salivary flow rate exhibits circadian variation and peaks in mid-afternoon. Normal salivary flow rates are in the region of 0.3–0.4 ml/min when unstimulated and 1.5–2.0 ml/min when stimulated, although both rates have wide normal ranges (*see* Chapter 3). Approximately 0.5–0.6 litres of saliva is secreted per day. The contribution of the different glands to whole saliva varies according to the level of stimulation. For unstimulated saliva, about 25% comes from the parotid glands, 60% from the submandibular glands, 7–8% from the sublingual gland and 7–8% from the minor mucous glands. During sleep, flow rate is negligible. For highly stimulated saliva the contribution from the parotids increases to an estimated 50%, the submandibulars contribute 35%, the sublinguals 7–8% and 7–8% comes from the minor mucous glands.

Many drugs used for the treatment of common conditions such as hypertension, depression and allergies (to mention but a few), also influence salivary flow rate and composition. Factors influencing salivary flow rate and composition are considered in more detail in Chapter 3.

The determination of a patient's salivary flow rate is a simple procedure. Both unstimulated and stimulated flow rates can be measured and changes in flow can be monitored over time. Measurement of salivary flow is considered further in Chapters 3 and 4. Other clinical investigations of salivary function such as sialography and scintiscanning require referral for specialist evaluation.

Table 1.2 The average composition of unstimulated and stimulated human whole saliva

	Unstimulated	Stimulated
Water	99.4%	99.5%
Solids	0.6%	0.5%
Flow rate (ml/min)	0.3–0.4	1.0–3.0
pH	5.7–7.1	Up to 7.8
Inorganic constituents	**Range**	**Range**
Sodium (mmol/l)	2–26	13–80
Potassium (mmol/l)	13–40	13–38
Calcium (mmol/l)	0.5–2.8	0.2–4.7
Magnesium (mmol/l)	0.15–0.6	0.2–0.6
Chloride (mmol/l)	8–40	10–56
Hydrogen carbonate (mmol/l)	0.1–8.0	4–40
Phosphate (mmol/l)	2–22	1.5–25
Thiocyanate (mmol/l)	0.4–5.0	0.4–3.0
Iodide (μmol/l)	2–22	2–30
Fluoride (μmol/l)	0.2–2.8	0.8–6.3

Saliva as a diagnostic fluid

Caries risk assessment

A number of caries risk assessment tests based on measurements in saliva have been developed. Examples are tests that measure salivary *Mutans streptococci* and lactobacilli and salivary buffering capacity. High levels of *Mutans streptococci*, ie >10^6 colony forming units (CFUs) per ml of saliva, are associated with an increased risk of developing caries. High levels of lactobacilli (>10^6 CFUs per ml saliva) are found amongst individuals with frequent carbohydrate consumption and are also associated with an increased risk of caries. Buffering capacity is a measure of the host's ability to neutralize the reduction in plaque pH produced by acidogenic organisms. Although many efforts have been made to identify a test or combination of tests to predict caries development, no one test has been found to predict this multifactorial disease accurately. In fact, past caries history in the primary and permanent dentitions is presently the best indicator of caries susceptibility. However, the salivary tests are useful indicators

Table 1.2 (continued) The average composition of unstimulated and stimulated human whole saliva

Organic constituents	Unstimulated	Stimulated
Protein (g/l)	1.7	1.0–6.4
Serum albumin (mg/l)		25
Gamma globulins (mg/l)		50
Mucoproteins (g/l)		0.45
MUC5B (mg/l)	850	400
MUC7 (mg/l)	80	40
Amylase (g/l)		0.42
Lysozyme (g/l)		0.14
Proline-rich proteins (mg/l)	0–80	
Lactoferrin		
Carbonic anhydrase		
Fibronectin (mg/l)	0.2–2.0	
Statherin (mg/l)	16–147	
Carbohydrate (g/l)		0.27–0.40
Blood group substances (mg/l)		10–20
Glucose (mmol/l)		0.02–0.17
Lipids (mg/l)		20
Cortisol (nmol/l)		2–20
Amino acids (mg/l)		40
Urea (mmol/l)		2.0–4.20
Ammonia (mmol/l)		0.6–7.0

Cells are blank where quantitative data are not available. Adapted from Ferguson (1999), page 136.

of caries susceptibility at the individual level where they can be used for prospective monitoring of caries preventive interventions and for profiling of patient disease susceptibility.

A number of salivary variables measured for caries risk assessment in dentistry are listed in Table 1.3.

Some of these variables are more accessible to the practitioner for measurement than others. Whole salivary flow rates are easily measured although due attention must be paid to the conditions under which saliva is collected. Because of the circadian rhythm of salivary flow rate, repeated measurements should be made at the same time of day, (for details of method of measurement of resting and stimulated flow rates see Chapter 3). Buffering

Table 1.3 Salivary variables measured for caries risk assessment

Variable	Caries risk assessment
Flow rate	At extremes of flow, flow rate is related to caries activity. Low flow rate is associated with increased caries and high flow rate is related to reduced caries risk.
Buffering capacity	Higher buffering capacity indicates better ability to neutralize acid and therefore more resistance to demineralization.
Salivary *Mutans streptococci*	$>10^6$ CFU/ml saliva indicates increased risk.
Salivary lactobacilli	$>10^6$ CFU/ml saliva indicates frequent carbohydrate consumption and therefore increased risk.
Fluoride ions	Higher levels of fluoride ions in saliva are associated with use of fluoride products or with water fluoridation.
Ca and P ions	Higher levels associated with less caries.

capacity is easily measured at the chair side using a commercially available kit. Paraffin-wax-stimulated saliva samples are used for bacteriological tests as chewing dislodges the flora into the saliva. Mutans streptococci and lactobacilli may both be cultured from stimulated saliva samples. Commercially available chair side tests also facilitate their measurement. The biochemical measurement of fluoride, calcium and phosphate requires special laboratory facilities, which are not readily available to the practitioner.

General diagnostics
Saliva is easily available for non-invasive collection and analysis. It can be used to monitor the presence and level of hormones, drugs, antibodies, micro-organisms and ions. It can be particularly useful where there are problems with venipuncture; for example where study logistics require repeated sampling, which makes venipuncture uncomfortable or unacceptable. In many instances collections of whole saliva are easiest and most acceptable. Developments in this important area of diagnostics are still at an early stage and many of the uses listed below are in the early stages of development.

Analysis of saliva has been employed in:

- Pharmacokinetics, therapeutic drug monitoring of some drugs and metabolic studies.

- Monitoring of a number of drugs: theophylline, lithium, phenytoin and carbamazepine, cortisol, digoxin and ethanol.

- Testing for drugs of abuse.

- Evaluation and assessment of endocrine studies.

- Testosterone in the male.

- Progesterone in the female.

- Diagnostic immunology – virus diagnosis and surveillance (eg antibodies against the measles, rubella and mumps viruses).

- Diagnosis of graft-versus-host disease.

- Screening tests.

Further Reading

1   Ferguson D B. *Oral Bioscience*. Churchill Livingstone, 1999.
2   Malamud D, Tabak L, Eds. *Saliva as a Diagnostic Fluid*. New York: New York Academy of Sciences, 1995.
3   Nauntofte B, Tenovuo J O, Lagerlöf F. Secretion and Composition of Saliva. *In* Fejerskov O, Kidd E A M (Eds) *Dental Caries The Disease and its Clinical Management*. Chapter 2. pp7-27. Oxford: Blackwell Munksgaard, 2003.
4   Norman J E de B, McGurk M, Eds. *Colour Atlas of Salivary Gland Diseases and Surgery*. London: Mosby-Wolfe, 1995.

2 Mechanisms of salivary secretion

Peter M Smith

Introduction

The key to understanding the mechanism of salivary secretion is in identifying the individual components of the secretory process and in visualizing how these components fit together. Difficulties in understanding arise because there are a lot of components and more than one way of assembling them.

Salivary secretion may be defined as '*A unidirectional movement of fluid, electrolytes and macromolecules into saliva in response to appropriate stimulation*'. This simple statement encapsulates most aspects of the secretory process and points towards what is probably the most important and topical aspect of secretory physiology. The critical words in the statement are *stimulation, fluid* and *electrolytes, macromolecules* and finally *unidirectional*.

Stimulation encompasses the neural mechanisms that integrate the response to salivary stimuli, such as taste, and the processes within each salivary acinar cell that communicate between the nervous system and the secretory machinery.

Fluid, electrolytes and *macromolecules* describe defining components of saliva. The unique viscoelastic and antibacterial properties of saliva stem largely from its protein component. The electrolyte content adds acid buffering and remineralization capabilities and the fluid vehicle dilutes and clears the oral environment (see chapters on clearance, functions of salivary proteins and saliva and mineral equilibrium).

The only way to achieve a *unidirectional* movement of fluid, electrolytes and macromolecules across a cell is if one end of the cell behaves differently from the other. It has always been obvious that one end of a secretory acinar cell looks different from the other; what is much less obvious is that this polarity extends to every aspect of cell function, including the control of secretion.

Stimulation

Neural control of salivation

The neural control of secretion is outlined in Figure 2.1. The primary stimulus for salivation is taste[1] and afferent input is carried to the solitary nucleus in the medulla via the facial (VII) and glossopharyngeal (IX) nerves. Input from mastication and from other senses, such as smell, sight and thought are also integrated in the solitary nucleus. In man, taste and mastication are by far the most important stimuli of salivary secretion. Parasympathetic efferent pathways for the sublingual and submandibular glands are from the facial nerve via the submandibular ganglion and for the parotid gland from the glossopharyngeal nerve via the otic ganglion. These pathways regulate fluid secretion by releasing acetylcholine (ACh) at the surface of the salivary gland acinar cells. Macromolecule secretion is regulated by noradrenalin (NorAd or norepinephrine, USA) release from sympathetic nerves. Sympathetic post-ganglionic pathways are from the cervical ganglion of the sympathetic chain. The division between parasympathetic and sympathetic control of different aspects of the secretory process is blurred slightly because parasympathetic

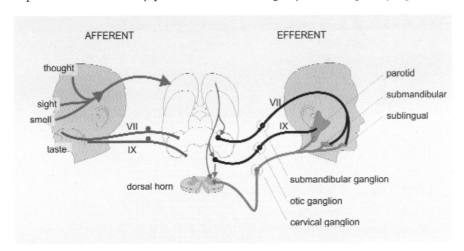

Fig. 2.1 The first step in stimulus-secretion coupling is release of a neurotransmitter. Afferent pathways: taste; facial (VII) and glossopharyngeal (IX) nerves to solitary nucleus in the medulla. Also input from higher centres in response to smell, etc. Efferent pathways: parasympathetic; sublingual and submandibular from facial nerve via submandibular ganglion. Parotid from glossopharyngeal via otic ganglion. Sympathetic post-ganglionic from cervical ganglion of sympathetic chain.

nerves may also release peptides, such as substance P and vasoactive intestinal polypeptide (VIP) and, NorAd will also bind to Ca^{2+}-mobilizing α-adrenergic receptors.[2]

Second messengers

Second messengers carry the secretory stimulus from the nerves into the secretory cells and provide a flexible coupling between the intracellular and extracellular environments with built-in amplification. Amplification is one of the most significant aspects of 2nd messenger signalling because it transduces a very small extracellular stimulus into a large intracellular event.[3]

As shown in Figure 2.2, fluid secretion is activated by binding of ACh to muscarinic M3 receptors, macromolecule secretion by binding of NorAd to β adrenergic receptors. Both of these receptors belong to the seven membrane-spanning domain G-protein-linked receptor superfamily. Ligand binding (a

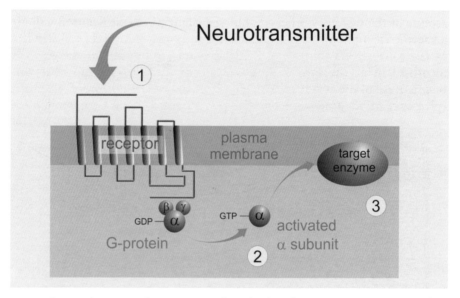

Fig. 2.2 The second step in stimulus-secretion coupling is binding of neurotransmitter to receptor and activation of an intracellular enzyme. Members of the seven membrane-spanning domain superfamily of receptors are linked to heterotrimeric G-proteins. On activation by neurotransmitter (1), the G-protein binds GTP instead of GDP and is thus activated. The α subunit of the activated G-protein dissociates from the $\beta\gamma$ subunits (2) and binds to and activates a target enzyme (3).

ligand may be defined as something which binds with high specificity to a particular receptor) to members of this family of receptors causes activation of an associated heterotrimeric G-protein by replacement of bound GDP with GTP. The activated α-subunit of the G-protein dissociates from the βγ subunits and in turn activates a target enzyme.[4] The target enzyme in fluid secretion is phospholipase C (PLC, activated by G-α_q) and in protein secretion adenylate cyclase (activated by G-α_s). The G-protein α subunit is self inactivating because it has an intrinsic GTPase activity. Once GTP is hydrolysed to GDP the α subunit and the enzyme it has activated switch off again. Nevertheless, the relatively slow rate of GTP hydrolysis means that a single activated target enzyme can process many molecules of substrate before it inactivates.

Adenylate cyclase and cyclic-AMP

The next and all subsequent steps in macromolecule secretion are regulated by cyclic-AMP (cAMP). While Figure 2.2 shows the general process whereby receptor activation is linked to activation of a 'target enzyme', Figure 2.3 shows a specific example where the 'target enzyme' is adenylate cyclase. Adenylate cyclase converts ATP into cAMP. Cyclic AMP was the first 2nd messenger to be identified; in fact the term '2nd Messenger' was coined to describe the actions of cAMP. All of the activities of cAMP are mediated through protein kinase A (pKA or cAMP-dependent protein kinase). At rest, pKA is a tetramer composed

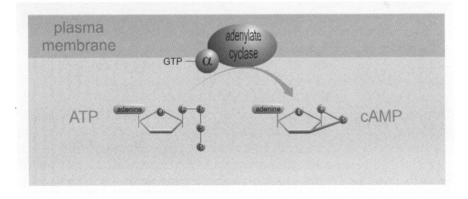

Fig. 2.3 The third step in macromolecule stimulus-secretion coupling is production of cAMP. Adenylate cyclase, activated by Gα_s converts ATP into cAMP.

of two catalytic subunits and two regulatory subunits. When cAMP binds to pKA, the catalytic subunits separate from the regulatory subunits and become active.[4] Protein kinase A (as its name suggests) phosphorylates proteins, not the proteins that comprise the macromolecule component of saliva but rather the cellular proteins responsible for its synthesis and secretion. Phosphorylation is a very common mechanism of upregulating the activity of cellular proteins. A characteristic of cAMP-dependent cellular processes is that upregulation depends not on increased activity of a single enzyme or process but rather on increased activity of many processes. Downregulation of cAMP-dependent processes, including macromolecule secretion, is accomplished by a reduction in cAMP levels mediated by the enzyme cAMP phosphodiesterase.[4] Phosphodiesterase activity is itself subject to many regulatory factors, including G-protein coupled receptor activation.

Phospholipase C, inositol 1,4,5 trisphosphate and calcium

The stimulus for fluid secretion, initiated by binding of ACh to muscarinic M3 receptors and activation of G-α_q and PLC, continues with the soluble product of PLC activity, inositol 1,4,5 trisphosphate (IP_3)[4], see Figure 2.4. IP_3 acts by binding to IP_3 receptors on endosomes, such as the endoplasmic reticulum (ER), and releasing the Ca^{2+} stored within. The Ca^{2+} content of the ER is maintained at a much higher concentration (~1 mM) than that of the cytoplasm (~100 nM) by Ca^{2+} ATPase activity so that activation of a Ca^{2+} channel is sufficient to raise cytosolic Ca^{2+} activity by diffusion from the Ca^{2+} stores. IP_3 receptors *are* Ca^{2+} channels, activated by IP_3 binding.[5]

IP_3 receptors are also sensitive to cytosolic Ca^{2+} activity and stay open for longer when $[Ca^{2+}]_i$ is raised. This property of the receptor can dramatically enhance the Ca^{2+} mobilizing properties of IP_3 by positive feedback or Ca^{2+}-induced Ca^{2+} release (CICR).[5] The Ca^{2+} signal may be further amplified by Ca^{2+} release through ryanodine receptors, a second Ca^{2+} channel also present on the ER of acinar cells.[6] Ryanodine receptors are also Ca^{2+} sensitive and contribute to CICR. The sensitivity of ryanodine receptors to Ca^{2+} may be 'set' by the cytosolic concentration of cyclic ADP ribose, a product of βNAD produced by ribosyl cyclase regulated by cyclic GMP and possibly nitric oxide levels.[6] The Ca^{2+} signal is therefore actively propagated through the acinar cell by an explosive release of Ca^{2+} from stores, triggered by IP_3, amplified by Ca^{2+} and carried by both IP_3 and ryanodine receptors (Fig. 2.5).[7]

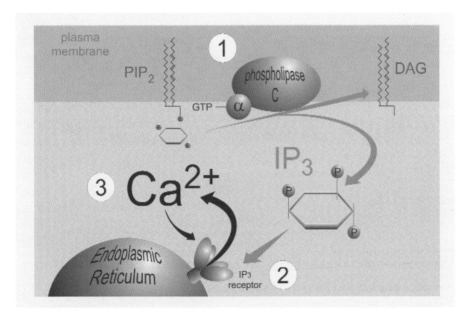

Fig. 2.4 The third step in fluid and electrolyte stimulus-secretion coupling is an increase in intracellular Ca^{2+} activity. Phospholipase C, activated by G-α_q splits phosphatidyl inositide 4,5, bisphosphate (PIP_2) into IP_3 and diacylglycerol (DAG)(1). IP_3 binds to and activates IP_3 receptors on the ER (2). Ca^{2+} diffuses from the ER into the cytoplasm. Increased $[Ca^{2+}]_i$ promotes activation of the IP_3 receptors and stimulates further Ca^{2+} mobilization (3).

In addition to mobilizing stored Ca^{2+}, the secretory process can also utilize extracellular Ca^{2+}. Ca^{2+} influx across the plasma membrane is stimulated by depletion of the intracellular Ca^{2+} stores by a mechanism that is still poorly understood, but which probably depends on conformational coupling between the IP_3 receptors and plasma membrane Ca^{2+} influx channels.[8] Downregulation of the Ca^{2+} signal depends mainly on Ca^{2+} ATPase activity to pump the Ca^{2+} back into the stores or out of the cell.

Macromolecules

Macromolecules cannot cross the plasma membrane. At first sight, this might seem to be an insurmountable problem for a protein-secreting cell but the secret to protein secretion is to synthesize proteins for export within endosomes (Fig. 2.6). Topologically at least, these proteins are never inside the cell and so

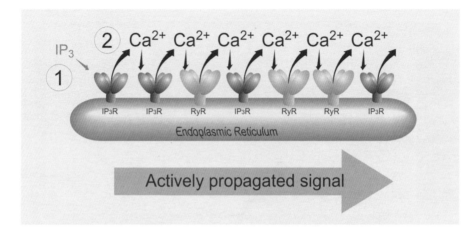

Fig. 2.5 Actively propagated Ca^{2+} signal. IP_3 stimulates Ca^{2+} release from IP_3 receptors (IP_3R). Ca^{2+} stimulates further Ca^{2+} release from IP_3R and from ryanodine receptors (RyR). Release of Ca^{2+} by one receptor triggers activation of the next and thus actively propagates the signal. Thus a Ca^{2+} signal may start at the apical pole of the cell and then rapidly become cell-wide.

do not have to cross the cell membrane to get out. Proteins are secreted when the endosome or vesicle into which they were synthesized fuses with the plasma membrane in the process of exocytosis.

Synthesis of secretory proteins begins with gene transcription and manufacture of messenger RNA to carry the sequence information from the nucleus to ribosomes in the cytoplasm. Secretory proteins start with a 'signal sequence' which targets the developing polypeptide to the ER where it is N-glycosylated and folded into the correct three-dimensional structure. Small membrane vesicles carry proteins from the ER through several layers of the golgi apparatus for additional processing and 'packaging' for export. Proteins move by default onwards from the ER; those destined to remain in the cell contain specific 'retention sequences' to segregate them from secretory proteins. Secretory proteins are concentrated within golgi-condensing vacuoles and stored in secretory vesicles. As these mature they are transported close to the apical membrane. In response to a secretory stimulus, secretory vesicles fuse with the plasma membrane and discharge their contents outside the cell.[1,9]

The secretory process may be divided into four stages. Synthesis, segregation and packaging, storage and release. Each of these stages is regulated by phosphorylation of target proteins by cAMP-dependent pKA.

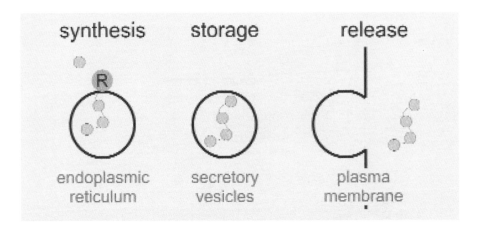

Fig. 2.6 Secretory proteins are synthesized in endosomes. Proteins are synthesized inside endosomes by ribosomes (R). Secretory vesicles mature and are stored until a secretory stimulus is received.

Therefore an increase in cAMP stimulates
- transcription of genes for salivary proteins (eg PRPs);

- post-translational modification (eg glycosylation);

- maturation and translocation of secretory vesicles to the apical membrane;

- exocytosis.

Thus, an increase in the level of cAMP within the cell will stimulate every step involved in protein secretion (Fig. 2.7).[2,10]

The role of cAMP in regulation of exocytosis in salivary acinar cells is unusual if not unique. Exocytosis is much more commonly regulated by Ca^{2+}, even in the functionally very similar pancreatic acinar cells.[11] Both second messengers have some regulatory function in all protein-secreting cells, but only in salivary glands does cAMP have such a central role. The molecular components of exocytosis have been extensively studied in other cell types and the key players, soluble N-ethylmaleimide-sensitive fusion protein attachment receptors (SNAREs) are also present in salivary gland acinar cells. It seems unlikely therefore that there is a fundamental difference in the mechanism of exocytosis between salivary gland cells and other cell types. Secretory vesicles have SNAREs (v-SNARES) which recognize plasma membrane SNARES

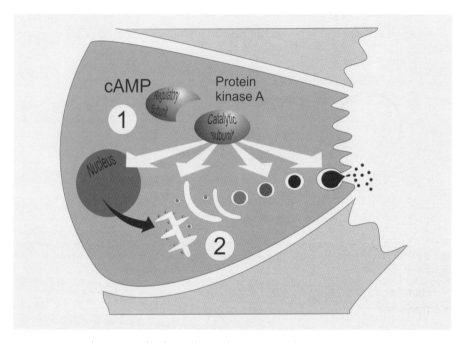

Fig. 2.7 cAMP and PKA. cAMP binding to the regulatory subunit of pKA releases and activates the catalytic subunit (1). The catalytic subunit phosphorylates and upregulates many components of the secretory pathway including exocytosis (2).

(t-SNARES) and the two form tight complexes that link the two membranes and mediate the three steps in regulated exocytosis; docking, priming and fusion (Fig. 2.8).[10] In neuronal cells, for example, secretory vesicles are docked and primed and await a Ca^{2+} signal to trigger exocytosis. Perhaps in salivary gland acinar cells, secretory vesicles wait for a secretory stimulus at an earlier cAMP-dependent 'brake' point.[10]

Not all secreted proteins originate in salivary gland cells. Saliva also contains plasma proteins, for example the immunoglobulin, IgA. IgA is no more able to cross the plasma membrane than any other protein and so crosses acinar cells in a membrane vesicle. Receptors for IgA on the basolateral membrane of the acinar cells bind IgA which is taken 'within' the cell by endocytosis. Following transcytosis of the vesicles containing IgA, the immunoglobulin is released into the saliva by exocytosis (Fig. 2.9).[12]

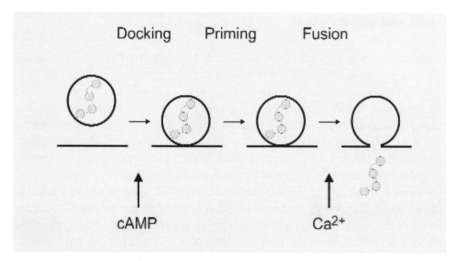

Fig. 2.8 A cAMP-dependent 'brake' point. Exocytosis occurs in three stages; docking, priming and fusion. The fusion process itself is Ca^{2+} dependent. However, earlier stages of the process, eg 'docking' could be cAMP dependent. In salivary gland cells, this step is the rate limiting 'brake' point in exocytosis.

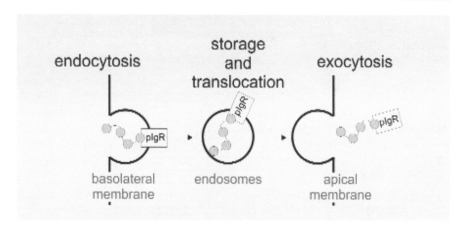

Fig. 2.9 Transcellular protein transport. Polymeric IgA and IgM are transported across salivary gland cells by the polymeric immunoglobulin receptor (pIgR). The pIgR binds its ligand at the basolateral surface and is internalized into endosomes. Here it is sorted into vesicles that transcytose it to the apical surface. At the apical surface the pIgR is proteolytically cleaved and the large extracellular fragment is released together with the ligand.

Fluid and electrolytes

Fluid secretion is inevitably a process with multiple steps because biological systems cannot *actively* transport fluid as such. The only way of moving fluid rapidly across a tissue is by osmosis. Therefore, as shown in Figure 2.10, fluid secreting tissues, including salivary acinar cells, concentrate electrolytes by active transport and the concentration gradient forces water to move. Throughout the salivary glands, there is in general only a single cell layer between the extracellular fluid and the lumen of the acinus or duct. Therefore, the processes of secretion and absorption involve transport across a single cellular layer.

Acinar cells use active transport to increase the Cl^- concentration inside the cell so that activation of an apical membrane Cl^- channel allows Cl^- to leave down its electrochemical gradient into the lumen of the acinus. Na^+ crosses the acinar cells to maintain electroneutrality and the movement of Na^+ and Cl^- create the osmotic gradient across the tissue and water follows. The pivotal step, the single step that determines whether or not a cell is secreting is activation

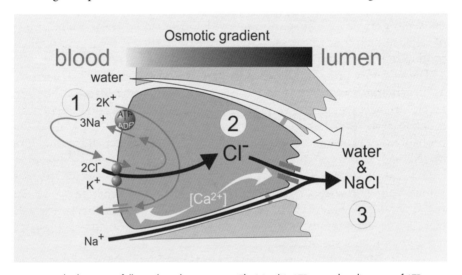

Fig. 2.10 Fluid secretion follows electrolyte secretion. The Na^+/K^+ ATPase makes direct use of ATP to pump Na^+ out of the cell and create an inwardly directed Na^+ gradient. This energizes the $Na^+/K^+/2Cl^-$ cotransport system (1) which in turn concentrates Cl^- above its electrochemical potential (2). Increased $[Ca^{2+}]_i$ opens the Ca^{2+}-dependent K^+ and Cl^- channels and Cl^- crosses the apical membrane into the lumen of the acinus (2). Na^+ follows Cl^- across the cell to maintain electroneutrality and the resultant osmotic gradient moves water (3).

of the apical membrane Cl^- channel. This step is regulated by increased $[Ca^{2+}]_i$. A cell-wide increase in $[Ca^{2+}]_i$ will also activate the basolateral K^+ channel which keeps the membrane potential at a high negative value and thus preserves the driving force for Cl^- efflux.

Fluid secreted by electrolyte-led transport is always isotonic. Once isotonicity is reached, there is no additional driving force for water movement. The ability of salivary glands to generate an hypotonic saliva lies with the striated ducts. Striated duct cells pump electrolytes from the primary saliva by active transport. At first sight, it might seem that this will simply reverse the secretory process, but the striated ducts are impermeable to water, so there can be no osmotically driven water reabsorption. The basic outline of this secretory process was identified as the 'two stage hypothesis' by Thaysen *et al* in 1954. The fluid secretory process in the acinar cells has a much greater capacity than the electrolyte reabsorptive process in the ducts. This is why the composition of saliva changes with flow rate. At low, unstimulated, flow rates, saliva moves slowly through the ducts and the striated ducts are able to modify the composition of the saliva substantially. At high, stimulated, flow rates, the saliva passes rapidly through the ducts with little alteration. The composition of saliva at high flow rates more closely resembles that of the primary saliva produced by the acinar cells.

The secretory process for bicarbonate is similar to that for Cl^- inasmuch as bicarbonate is concentrated within acinar cells and released following receipt of a secretory stimulus. Details of the process for bicarbonate are much less well understood than for Cl^-. In most salivary glands, uptake is probably via a carbonic anhydrase mediated process that depends ultimately on Na^+/H^+ exchange and the Na^+ gradient. Efflux is probably via a bicarbonate permeable channel (Fig. 2.11). The Ca^{2+}-dependent Cl^- channel is bicarbonate permeable and bicarbonate efflux via this channel would be the simplest mechanism for bicarbonate secretion. Qualitatively at least, bicarbonate secretion would be as effective as Cl^- secretion as a mechanism for driving fluid movement.[2]

Bicarbonate is one of the electrolytes reabsorbed by the striated ducts and the bicarbonate concentration in unstimulated saliva is consequently low. A failure to reabsorb bicarbonate at high flow rates is the simplest explanation for the much higher bicarbonate concentration in stimulated saliva.

Acinar cells secrete macromolecules and fluid and electrolytes. Striated duct cells reabsorb electrolytes. Intercalated ducts lie between the acini and the

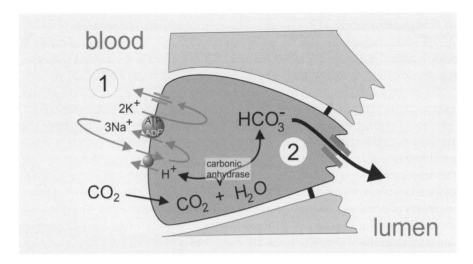

Fig. 2.11 Bicarbonate secretion. Carbon dioxide inside cells is converted to HCO_3^- and H^+ by carbonic anhydrase. HCO_3^- is secreted across the apical membrane of the cell through an anion channel (2). H^+ are actively extruded across the basolateral membrane by Na^+/H^+ exchange energized by the Na^+ gradient which is created by the action of the Na^+/K^+ ATPase (1). If protons were not lost from the cell, carbonic anhydrase would be unable to generate HCO_3^-.

striated ducts and seem to function more like acinar cells than striated duct cells. They probably make little contribution to protein secretion but may have an important role in bicarbonate and fluid secretion.

Water channels

There are two possible routes for water to take across the cell, either through the tight junctions between the cells (paracellular) or across both the apical and basolateral membranes (transcellular). There has been much discussion as to which is the dominant route and little evidence to distinguish absolutely between them.[13] The intrinsic water permeability of the plasma membrane is very low and both apical and basolateral membranes must therefore contain water channels to facilitate transcellular water transport. Water channels in salivary acinar cells are members of the aquaporin (AQP) family. Aquaporins are membrane proteins composed of four subunits, each of which has six membrane-spanning domains that form a water-permeable pore. Aquaporins come in two types, one of which transports only water and another which is also permeable to glycerol. Neither type conducts ions.[14] There are at least 10 mammalian aquaporin isoforms and

AQP5 has been localized to the apical membrane of salivary gland acinar cells. AQP5 knockout mice (genetically modified mice that cannot produce AQP5) show a 60% reduction in stimulated flow in airway mucosal glands, which would suggest that at least this proportion of water flow is transcellular.[15]

Unidirectional

In any normal circumstance the secretory process works only one way. The unidirectionality of secretion is achieved by the barrier function of the acinar and duct cells in separating extracellular fluid from saliva and, at a cellular level, by polarization of structure (Fig. 2.12) and function. Every cell type involved in salivary secretion is polarized in one way or another. Acinar and duct cells are connected together by tight junctions, which also form the division between the apical membrane which faces into the lumen of the gland and the basolateral membrane which faces the extracellular fluid. The different properties of these two membranes are fundamental to the polarization of cell function necessary for unidirectional secretion.

Striated ducts are so called because in longitudinal section, their basolateral side has a striped appearance. The stripes are caused by many infoldings of the

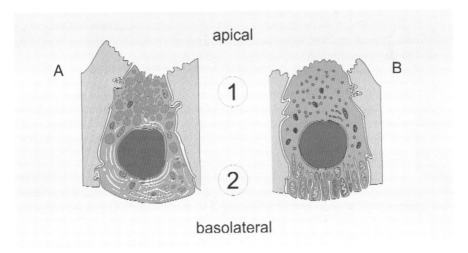

Fig. 2.12 Histological polarity. Acinar and striated ducts are very obviously polarized. Acinar cells (A) have a high density of secretory vesicles at the apical pole (1) and striated duct cells (B) have basal infoldings and a high density of mitochondria (2).

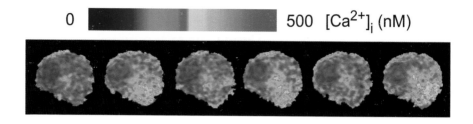

Fig. 2.13 Local Ca^{2+} signals. Sequential Ca^{2+} image maps taken over 20 s of a single mouse submandibular acinar cell loaded with the Ca^{2+} sensitive dye fura-2 and stimulated with 20 nM ACh. The Ca^{2+} signal manifests only at the apical pole, at the bottom of the image. Each Ca^{2+} response lasted <500 ms.

basal membrane, crammed full of mitochondria (Fig. 2.12). A high density of mitochondria, close to the plasma membrane is usually indicative of primary active transport, in this case the Na^+/K^+ ATPase. The most obvious defining feature of acinar cells is the apical pole of the cell, densely packed with secretory vesicles.

From a functional perspective, the apical pole of the acinar cells is where all the most critical events occur. Secretory vesicles are directed by the actin cytoskeleton towards the apical pole of the cell and exocytosis occurs almost exclusively at the apical pole.

The key event in fluid secretion, activation of the Ca^{2+}-dependent anion channel, also occurs at the apical pole. There is growing evidence to indicate that the controlling Ca^{2+} signal originates at the apical pole of the cell and in certain circumstances may be restricted to this pole of the cell (Fig. 2.13).[16]

Calcium signals are very 'expensive' in terms of the metabolic cost of holding $[Ca^{2+}]_i$ at nanomolar levels and, because sustained elevated Ca^{2+} levels are cytotoxic, potentially dangerous to the cell. Spatially restricted Ca^{2+} signals may be an elegant resolution to both of these problems. It has proved very challenging to elucidate the mechanisms underlying local Ca^{2+} signals, not least of all, how the cell stops the signal from propagating across the cell by CICR. A partial answer to this question may simply be that spatially restricted Ca^{2+} signals are very brief. The apical origin of the Ca^{2+} signal is slightly odd, given that the ER, which is thought to be the primary source of stored Ca^{2+}, is almost exclusively distributed through the basolateral region of the cell. Secretory vesicles, which have a very obvious apical location, have been proposed as a possible Ca^{2+} store.[17]

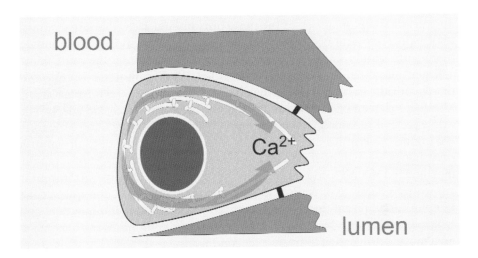

Fig. 2.14 Ca²⁺ tunnelling. Ca^{2+} is stored in the ER, most of which is at the basolateral pole of the cell. Nevertheless, Ca^{2+} signals originate at the apical pole of the cell. One possibility is that Ca^{2+} 'tunnels' through the ER from the basal pole to release sites at the apical pole. Think of it as plumbing for cells with a water tank in the roof (basal pole) and a tap in the kitchen (apical pole).

An alternative, and more widely accepted, mechanism depends on the reticulate nature of the ER. In this model, Ca^{2+} is stored at the basolateral pole of the cell and 'tunnels' through the ER to the apical pole where it is released (Fig. 2.14).[18] This last mechanism also offers the intriguing possibility that the actin cytoskeleton that shapes the dynamic structure of the ER and regulates transport of secretory vesicles to the secretory pole of the cell, might also have a role in the control of fluid secretion.[19]

Pharmacological control of fluid and electrolyte secretion

Every step of stimulus-secretion coupling is potentially vulnerable to dysfunction under pathological conditions. The challenge for secretory physiologists studying autoimmune hyposalivation conditions, such as Sjögren's syndrome, is to find the points at which the immune response could damage the secretory process.[20,21] There is a growing body of evidence to suggest that severe glandular atrophy is the end-stage of Sjögren's syndrome and that glandular hypofunction occurs much earlier in the pathology of the condition. Contrariwise, every step of stimulus-secretion coupling is a potential point for therapeutic intervention. Stimulation of fluid secretion by activation of muscarinic receptors is one of the more obvious and accessible entry points. Pilocarpine, a naturally occurring alkaloid, is probably the best known therapeutic cholinomimetic agent and is distributed under the trade name 'Salagen'. Cevimeline (Evoxac) is another cholinomimetic agent used therapeutically in the US which may have a higher specificity for muscarinic M3 receptors than pilocarpine and potentially, therefore fewer side-effects. The side-effects of therapeutic application of Salagan (15–30 mg/day) or Evoxac (90 mg/day), sweating, etc., are usually tolerated in preference to dry mouth (*see* Chapter 4). ACh itself is of little use therapeutically because it is so rapidly metabolized. Saliva production may be blocked by cholinergic receptor antagonists, such as atropine, which compete with ACh for muscarinic receptors and prevent the effects of parasympathetic stimulation on fluid and electrolyte secretion. The most common cause of dry mouth is as a side-effect of xerogenic drugs used to treat other conditions.

Microfluorimetry, electrophysiology and molecular biology are proving to be a powerful combination with which to study secretory mechanisms. For example: fluorescent probes for subcellular components, such as the ER, mitochondria or the nucleus may be used to visualize these organelles in living cells and determine their role in signal transduction. Caged agonists or second messengers may be used to provide precise spatial mapping of intracellular responses and so further refine our understanding of cellular polarization. Genes for key elements of the secretory machinery can be linked to fluorescent markers and expressed and visualized in isolated acinar cells by transient transfection. Gene knockouts can help pinpoint the function of specific proteins, such as AQP5 or ACh M3 receptors. There is now great scope and great potential in turning these powerful techniques towards understanding glandular pathologies.

References

1   Hector M P, Linden R W A. Reflexes of salivary secretion. *In* Garrett J R, Ekström J, Anderson LC (Eds) *Neural Mechanisms of Salivary Gland Secretion*, pp 196–217. Basel: Karger, 1999.
2   Turner R J, Sugiya H. Understanding salivary fluid and protein secretion. *Oral Dis* 2002; **8** : 3–11.
3   Rodbell M. Nobel Lecture. Signal transduction: evolution of an idea. *Biosci Rep* 1995; **15**: 117–33.
4   Hancock J T. *Cell Signalling*. pp 225. London: Longman, 1997.
5   Dawson A. IP(3) receptors. *Curr Biol* 2003; **13**: R424.
6   Galione A, Churchill G C. Interactions between calcium release pathways: multiple messengers and multiple stores. *Cell Calcium* 2002; **32**: 343–54.
7   Harmer A R, Gallacher D V, Smith P M. The role of Ins(1,4,5)P3, cADP-ribose and nicotinic acid adenine dinucleotide phosphate in Ca^{2+} signalling in mouse submandibular acinar cells. *Biochem J* 2001; **353**: 555–60.
8   Parekh A B, Penner R. Store depletion and calcium influx. *Physiol Rev* 1997; **77**: 901–30.

9 Garrett J R. Effects of Autonomic Nerve Stimulations on Salivary Parenchyma and Protein Secretion. *In* Garrett J R, Ekström J, Anderson L C (Eds) *Neural Mechanisms of Salivary Gland Secretion*. pp 59–79. Basel: Karger, 1999.

10 Fujita-Yoshigaki J. Divergence and convergence in regulated exocytosis: the characteristics of cAMP-dependent enzyme secretion of parotid salivary acinar cells. *Cell Signal* 1998; **10**: 371–5.

11 Wasle B, Edwardson J M. The regulation of exocytosis in the pancreatic acinar cell. *Cell Signal* 2002; **14**: 191–7.

12 Proctor G B et al. Salivary secretion of immunoglobulin A by submandibular glands in response to autonomimetic infusions in anaesthetised rats. *J Neuroimmunol* 2003; **136**: 17–24.

13 Loo D D, Wright E M, Zeuthen T. Water pumps. *J Physiol* 2002; **542**(Pt 1): 53–60.

14 Agre P et al. Aquaporin water channels – from atomic structure to clinical medicine. *J Physiol* 2002; **542**(Pt 1): 3–16.

15 Song Y, Verkman A S. Aquaporin-5 dependent fluid secretion in airway submucosal glands. *J Biol Chem* 2001; **276**: 41288–92.

16 Thorn P et al. Local and global cytosolic Ca^{2+} oscillations in exocrine cells evoked by agonists and inositol trisphosphate. *Cell* 1993; **74**: 661–8.

17 Marty A. Calcium release and internal calcium regulation in acinar cells of exocrine glands. *J Membr Biol* 1991; **124**: 189–97.

18 Petersen O H. Localization and regulation of Ca^{2+} entry and exit pathways in exocrine gland cells. *Cell Calcium* 2003; **33**: 337–44.

19 Harmer A R, Gallacher D V, Smith P M. Correlations between the functional integrity of the endoplasmic reticulum and polarised Ca^{2+} signalling in mouse lacrimal acinar cells: a role for inositol 1,3,4,5-tetrakisphosphate. *Biochem J* 2002; **367**: 137–43.

20 Dawson L J, Christmas S E, Smith P M. An investigation of interactions between the immune system and stimulus-secretion coupling in mouse submandibular acinar cells. A possible mechanism to account for reduced salivary flow rates associated with the onset of Sjogren's syndrome. *Rheumatology* 2000; **39**: 1226–33.

21 Dawson L J et al. Sjogren's syndrome – time for a new approach [editorial]. *Rheumatology* 2000; **39**: 234–7.

3

Factors influencing salivary flow rate and composition

C Dawes

This chapter covers the differences in flow rate and composition between unstimulated saliva (secreted continuously in the absence of exogenous stimulation) and stimulated saliva (secreted usually in response to masticatory or gustatory stimulation), the factors influencing salivary flow rate and composition, and their physiological importance.

Unstimulated saliva

Unstimulated whole saliva is the mixture of secretions that enter the mouth in the absence of exogenous stimuli such as tastants or chewing. It is composed of secretions from the parotid, submandibular, sublingual, and minor mucous glands but it also contains gingival crevicular fluid, desquamated epithelial cells, bacteria, leukocytes (mainly from the gingival crevice), and possibly food residues, blood and viruses. Unstimulated whole saliva is usually collected with the patient sitting quietly, with the head down and mouth slightly open to allow the saliva to drip from the lower lip into a beaker or similar receptacle over a given time, or the patient can spit out the saliva at regular intervals, while not swallowing. However, when saliva is spat out rather than drooled, the number of bacteria and epithelial cells is increased. The measured flow rate is actually the difference between the volume secreted by the different salivary glands and the volumes that may be lost by evaporation or mucosal absorption over the collection period.

Several large studies of unstimulated salivary flow rates in healthy individuals (Table 3.1) have found the average value for whole saliva to be about 0.3–0.4 ml/min, but the normal range is very large and includes individuals with very low flow rates who do not complain of a dry mouth.

Such a broad normal range makes it difficult to say whether or not a particular individual has an abnormally low flow rate. Unless saliva is almost completely absent, patients can be said to have a dry mouth (xerostomia) only on the basis of their subjective symptoms. However, a flow rate of <0.1 ml/min is considered objective evidence of hyposalivation.

Whether the flow rate is high or low is much less important than whether

Table 3.1 Unstimulated salivary flow rate (ml/min) in healthy individuals (for references see Dawes[3])

Studies	Type of saliva	Sample number	Mean (ml/min)	SD*
Andersson et al. (1974)	Whole	100	0.39	(0.21)
Becks and Wainwright (1943)	Whole	661	0.32	(0.23)
Heintze et al. (1983)	Whole	629	0.31	(0.22)
Shannon and Frome (1973)	Whole	50	0.32	(0.13)
Shannon (1967)	Parotid	4589	0.04	(0.03)
Enfors (1962)	Submandibular	54	0.10	(0.08)

* Note the very high standard deviation (SD) from the mean, indicating a very wide range of values covering normality.

it has changed adversely in a particular individual. Physicians will often take a patient's blood pressure as a yardstick for future measurements. Dentists, however, do not routinely measure the salivary flow rate, so that when a patient complains of having a dry mouth, it is impossible to judge whether or not a genuine reduction in flow has taken place. It would therefore be very advantageous if dentists included measurement of salivary flow as part of their regular examination. Just as there are individuals with very little saliva but without discomfort, so there are others with flow rates within the normal range who feel that their mouth is drowning in saliva. This problem is often due to difficulty in swallowing, rather than to a genuinely high flow rate.

Factors affecting the unstimulated salivary flow rate
Many factors influence the unstimulated salivary flow rate (Table 3.2).

Degree of hydration
This is potentially the most important factor. When body water content is reduced by 8%, the salivary flow rate decreases to virtually zero. For a person of about 70 kg, comprising about 50 kg of water, 8% dehydration means a loss of four litres. Smaller degrees of dehydration also decrease salivary flow while, in contrast, hyperhydration will increase the salivary flow rate.

Table 3.2 Factors affecting the unstimulated salivary flow rate in healthy subjects

Major factors*	Minor factors
Degree of hydration	Gender
Body position	Age (above 15 years)
Exposure to light	Body weight
Previous stimulation	Gland size
Smoking	Psychic effects
Circadian rhythms	- thought/sight of food
Circannual rhythms	- appetite
Drugs	- mental stress
	(Functional stimulation?)

*Most factors listed in the first column should be standardised during saliva collection

Body posture, lighting conditions, and smoking
Flow rate varies with position and a person when standing or lying will have a higher or lower flow rate, respectively, than when seated. Flow rate also decreases by 30–40% when subjects are blindfolded or in the dark. However, a study has shown that salivary flow is not less in blind subjects than in those with normal sight, which suggests that blind individuals eventually adapt to the lack of light entering the eyes. Olfactory stimulation and smoking cigarettes causes a temporary increase in the unstimulated salivary flow rate.

Biological rhythms
Circadian rhythms are rhythms with a period of about 24 h and include the rhythms in body temperature and in salivary flow.[1] The body temperature and the flow rate of saliva peak during the late afternoon (the acrophase) but the flow rate drops to almost zero during sleep (Fig. 3.1). It may therefore be important to standardize the time of day at which saliva is collected. This circadian rhythm also has important clinical implications for the timing of oral hygiene. The most important time to clean the teeth is probably at night before going to sleep, since the presence of plaque and food debris and a greatly reduced salivary flow during sleep provide optimum conditions for dental caries.

A study has also shown a circannual (about-yearly) rhythm in the flow rate

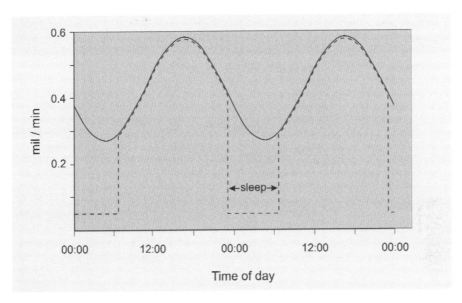

Fig. 3.1 The circadian rhythm in unstimulated salivary flow rate and the idealized effect of sleep (dashed line) from 2300 hours to 0700 hours (from Dawes[1]).

of parotid saliva, with a peak value in the winter. This study, carried out in Texas, found 35% lower flow rates in the summer, and it was assumed that the reduction then was due to dehydration. It would be interesting to repeat the study on subjects living in more temperate climates. Whether this finding means that people are more susceptible to caries in the summer than in the winter would be very hard to determine because full development of a caries lesion is such a long process, often taking several years.

Drugs
Many classes of drugs cause a reduction in salivary flow as a side-effect. They may act centrally or directly on the salivary glands (*see* Chapter 4).

Psychic stimuli
Thinking about food or seeing food are poor stimuli for salivation in humans. It may appear that one salivates at the thought of food, but it is more likely that one merely becomes aware of the pool of saliva present in the floor of the mouth between swallows. Although some researchers have measured a small rise in

Table 3.3 Stimulated salivary flow rates in man (for references see Dawes[3])

Authors	Type of saliva	Stimulus	Sample number	Mean (ml/min)	SD
Heintze et al. (1983)	Whole	Paraffin wax	629	1.6	(2.1)
Shannon and Frome (1973)	Whole	Chewing gum	200	1.7	(0.6)
Shannon et al. (1974)	Parotid	Grape candy	368	1.0	(0.5)
Mason et al. (1975)	Parotid	Lemon juice	169	1.5	(0.8)
Ericson et al. (1972)	Submandibular	1% citric acid	28	0.8	(0.4)

salivary flow with visual stimuli, others have found no effect. In general, therefore, thinking about or seeing food has little effect in stimulating salivary flow.

Functional stimulation
Further studies are needed to clarify whether regular stimulation of salivary flow, as by use of chewing gum, leads to an increase in the unstimulated flow rate, although there is evidence that it increases the stimulated flow rate (see later).

Stimulated saliva

This type of saliva is secreted in response to masticatory or gustatory stimulation, or to other less common stimuli such as certain drugs (eg pilocarpine) or to activation of the vomiting centre. Several studies of stimulated salivary flow rates have been done in healthy populations and show a wide variation among individuals (Table 3.3). The studies used a variety of stimuli, however, and international agreement on a suitable stimulus for experimental use would greatly help comparison of results from different studies.

Factors influencing the stimulated flow rate
Many factors (Table 3.4) influence the stimulated salivary flow rate, which, for whole saliva, has an average maximum value of about 7 ml/min.
Mechanical stimuli

Table 3.4 Factors affecting the flow of stimulated saliva

Nature of stimulus (mechanical, gustatory)	Smoking
Gag reflex	Unilateral stimulation
Vomiting	Gland size
Olfaction	Food intake

The action of chewing, in the absence of any taste (see results for gum-base in Fig. 3.2), will itself stimulate salivation but to a lesser degree than maximum gustatory stimulation with citric acid. Surprisingly, empty clenching of the teeth does not lead to an increase in salivary flow rate. Mastication also serves to mix the contents of the mouth, thus increasing slightly the distribution of the

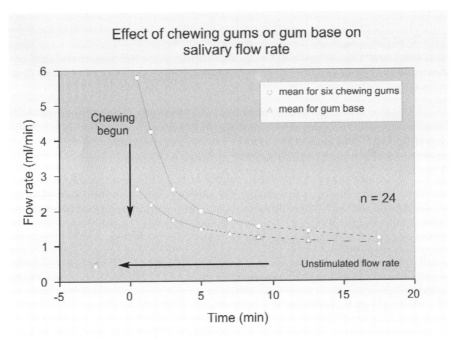

Fig. 3.2 Effect of six chewing gums and gum–base on the flow rate of whole saliva. Unstimulated saliva was collected for five minutes prior to chewing gum or gum–base stimulation, which began at time zero.

different types of saliva around the mouth. Mechanical stimulation of the fauces (the gag reflex) leads to increased salivation.

Vomiting
Salivary flow is increased just prior to and during vomiting. Unfortunately, the increased buffering power of the saliva secreted at the increased flow rate is inadequate to protect the teeth against the erosion caused by the acid gastric juice, particularly in individuals with chronic bulimia.

Gustatory and olfactory stimuli
Acid is the most potent of the four basic taste stimuli, the other three being salt, bitter and sweet. A study done with various concentrations of citric acid found that 5% citric acid stimulated a mean maximum salivary flow rate of about 7 ml/min.[7] The citric acid was continuously infused into the mouth, and the teeth were covered with a paraffin film to protect them against the acid. For a clinical evaluation of the residual secretory capacity in patients with hyposalivation, a 3% citric acid solution can be applied to the patient's tongue at regular intervals, so that the degree of stimulation is relatively standardized. If a gustatory stimulus is held in the mouth without movement, salivary flow decreases to the unstimulated rate with a halftime of about 11 seconds. However, if the gustatory stimulus is moved around to activate fresh taste receptors, the higher flow rate can be maintained.

For research purposes, sour candies (sweets) can be used to standardize the stimulated flow rate from cannulated individual glands. The patient collects saliva into a graduated test tube in front of a mirror. With the aid of a stopwatch, the patient can observe the salivary flow rate, and adjust it by changing the intensity of sucking on the candy. Standardization of flow rate allows study of the effect of other variables on salivary composition.

Olfactory stimuli and tobacco smoking, in comparison with gustatory stimuli, have relatively small effects in stimulating salivary flow.

Unilateral stimulus
If a person habitually chews on one side of the mouth, most of the saliva will be produced by the glands on that side, unless gustatory stimulation is also present.

Gland size
Maximum stimulated flow rate from a single gland is directly related to gland size. The unstimulated flow rate, however, is independent of gland size.

Age
Salivary flow is unrelated to age above 15 years. For a long time it was believed that salivary flow decreased with age, because such studies had been done on institutionalized, medicated patients. More recent research has shown that ageing has little effect on either the unstimulated or stimulated flow rate in normal healthy people who are not on medication. This is surprising because histological studies of salivary glands have shown a reduction in the proportion of secretory cells with age. Presumably there is normally a surplus of secretory tissue. However, many elderly people receive medication and the greater the number of drugs taken, the greater is the tendency for reduction in salivary flow.

Food intake
Surprisingly, very few studies have been carried out with food as the secretory stimulus. One study[7] tested the effects of seven foods. Even the most bland food (boiled rice) elicited 43% of the maximum flow rate produced by 5% citric acid. Rhubarb pie, which is both acidic and sweet, elicited 70% of the maximum flow rate. Further study showed that it was the gustatory stimulus provided by the food, rather than the mechanical stimulus of chewing, which was mainly responsible for these relatively high flow rates.

With chewing gum (Fig. 3.2), the flow rate is high initially but after about 10 minutes, as the flavour and sweeteners leach out and only the gum-base remains, it falls to the rate obtained by chewing gum-base alone, namely to two to three times the unstimulated rate. This increase in salivary flow during gum chewing can be maintained for as long as two hours and this may be very beneficial to those with a dry mouth.

Salivary flow rate and oral health
The unstimulated flow rate is more important than the stimulated flow for oral comfort, since only a small fraction of the day (54 minutes in a group of dental students) is spent eating. However, stimulation of the glands through mastication is beneficial in terms of promoting clearance of food from the mouth (*see* Chapter 5) and may help by causing an increase in the unstimulated flow rate, although

further studies of this are needed. A recent study by Simons *et al.*[6] has shown that two sugar-free chewing gums, one containing chlorhexidine, used by a group of 'frail, elderly', dentate subjects over a one-year period, led to improved oral health and a statistically significant 55–100% increase in their stimulated flow rate. This suggests that if the glands are stimulated regularly, their secretory ability may increase. Unfortunately, unstimulated flow rates were not measured in that study.

Carbohydrate clearance from the oral cavity

One major role of saliva is the clearance of carbohydrate from the mouth (*see* Chapter 5). The more rapid the flow, the faster the carbohydrate is cleared. This is true whether the saliva is unstimulated or stimulated, for example by chewing gum. If the gum contains sweeteners such as xylitol or sorbitol, which are minimally metabolized by plaque bacteria, then the increased salivary flow will be very effective in clearance of cariogenic carbohydrates.

Total daily salivary flow

If the average unstimulated flow rate over a waking period of 16 hours is about 0.3 ml/min, the total volume will be about 300 ml of saliva. During sleep, the maximum flow will fall to less than 0.1 ml/min, producing less than 40 ml of saliva in 7 hours. The average time spent eating each day has been estimated as 54 minutes and studies with various foods suggested that during eating the average stimulated flow rate is about 4 ml/min.[7] So about 200 ml of saliva per day will be produced during meals. Thus the total daily flow of saliva amounts to about 500–600 ml/24 h,[7] which is much less than the 1500 ml/24 h quoted in many textbooks.

The composition of saliva

The composition of saliva is affected by many factors (Table 3.5), such as the type of salivary gland producing the saliva. For example, most of the amylase in saliva is produced by the parotid glands while blood-group substances are derived mainly from the minor mucous glands.

Factors affecting salivary composition

Contribution of different glands

The parotid glands normally contribute about 25% of the total volume of unstimulated saliva, while the submandibular glands contribute 60%, the

Table 3.5 Factors affecting salivary composition

Species	Hormones
Glandular source	Pregnancy
Flow rate	Genetic polymorphism
Duration of stimulation	Antigenic stimulus
Previous stimulation	Exercise
Biological rhythms	Drugs
Nature of stimulus	Various diseases
Plasma composition (diet)	

sublingual 7–8%, and the minor mucous glands 7–8%. At very high stimulated flow rates, the parotid becomes the dominant gland, contributing about 50% of the whole saliva.

Flow Rate
The main factor affecting the composition of saliva is the flow rate (Fig. 3.3). As the flow rate increases, the pH and concentrations of some constituents rise (eg protein, sodium, chloride, bicarbonate), while those of others fall (eg magnesium and phosphate). The fluoride concentration in saliva is about 1 μmol/l (0.019 ppm) and is relatively independent of flow rate but with a slight increase at low unstimulated flow rates.

Duration of stimulation
When the salivary flow rate is held constant, the composition of the saliva depends on the duration of stimulation. So saliva collected at a constant flow rate for two minutes will have a different composition from saliva collected at the same flow rate for 10–15 minutes. For instance, the bicarbonate concentration increases progressively with duration of stimulation, whereas the chloride level, after an initial rise, falls in a reciprocal manner. The salivary composition will also vary depending on whether the gland has been stimulated during the previous hour.

Nature of the stimulus
Different stimuli have an effect on salivary composition, mainly because of their effect on the rate of flow. When the four basic taste stimuli (salt, acid,

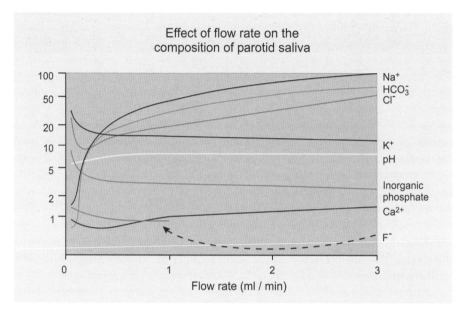

Effect of flow rate on the composition of parotid saliva

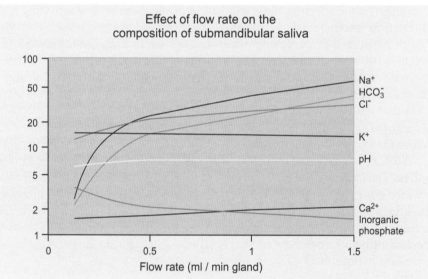

Effect of flow rate on the composition of submandibular saliva

Fig. 3.3 The effects of flow rate and duration of stimulation on the concentrations (mmol/l, except for F which is in μmol/l) of some components of (a) parotid saliva and (b) submandibular saliva.

bitter and sweet) were tested under constant-flow conditions, the type of stimulus used had virtually no effect on the electrolyte composition of parotid saliva, but the taste of salt elicited significantly higher protein content than with the other stimuli. There does not seem to be any physiological reason why this should be so. The increase occurred with all protein components; different stimuli did not elicit secretion of different proteins.

Acid is the most potent stimulus for salivary secretion and leads to production of an alkaline saliva. At one time it was thought that this was a beneficial adaptation to the nature of the stimulus. However, it is now known that the pH of saliva is dependent mainly on the flow rate and is independent of the nature of the stimulus.

Circadian rhythms
As with flow rate, salivary composition shows rhythms of high amplitude.[1] For instance, sodium and chloride levels peak in the early morning, while the rhythm in potassium concentration is 12 hours out of phase. The peak protein concentration is in the late afternoon. Thus for longitudinal studies, it may be important to standardize the time of saliva collection.

Saliva and taste
When saliva is first secreted by the acinar cells of the salivary glands, its electrolyte composition resembles that of an ultrafiltrate of plasma. As the saliva passes down the salivary duct, the gland expends energy to reabsorb virtually all the sodium chloride and most of the bicarbonate, while secreting potassium (Fig. 3.4). By the time the salivary secretion reaches the opening of the main excretory duct into the mouth its osmotic pressure is only about one-sixth of those in plasma and in the acinar cells.

Why do the salivary glands go to so much trouble to produce hypotonic saliva? The probable reason is to facilitate taste. Taste buds rapidly adapt to the taste of any solution in the mouth including, of course, saliva. Thus, if saliva had the same salt concentration as plasma (which is very high), we would be unable to taste salt concentrations lower than that in plasma. Hence the reabsorption of sodium and chloride during saliva production, and the resultant hypotonicity of saliva, facilitate our ability to taste salt.

Unstimulated saliva is particularly well adapted to facilitate our ability to taste low concentrations of substances with one of the four taste qualities of salt, sweet, acid or bitter. Besides being low in sodium and chloride (salt),

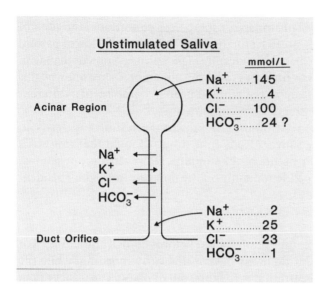

Unstimulated Saliva

Acinar Region

	mmol/L
Na⁺	145
K⁺	4
Cl⁻	100
HCO₃⁻	24 ?

Na⁺
K⁺
Cl⁻
HCO₃⁻

Duct Orifice

Na⁺	2
K⁺	25
Cl⁻	23
HCO₃⁻	1

Fig. 3.4 Changes in some electrolyte concentrations as unstimulated parotid saliva moves down the salivary duct.

unstimulated saliva is also low in glucose (sweet), buffering capacity (acid) and urea (bitter). Taste recognition threshold concentrations for NaCl, HCl, $NaHCO_3$, sucrose and urea are compared with the appropriate concentration levels in plasma and in unstimulated saliva in Table 3.6. It is only the concentrations of sodium and chloride in plasma that are higher than the taste recognition thresholds.

The buffering ability of saliva

Proteins

The concentration of protein in saliva is only about one-thirtieth of that in plasma, so that too few amino acids are present to have a significant buffering effect at the usual pH of the oral cavity. The buffering of dental plaque is discussed in Chapter 6 and the different proteins in saliva are discussed in Chapter 7.

Phosphate

As with proteins, there is too little phosphate in saliva to act as a significant buffer. Although the phosphate concentration in unstimulated whole saliva is about 6 mmol/l, the pH of the saliva is less than the pK_2 value of 7.2 for phosphate, making the phosphate ineffective as a buffer.

Table 3.6 Relation of plasma and saliva compositions* to taste thresholds

	Salt		Sour		Sweet	Bitter
	Na$^+$	Cl$^-$	H$^+$	HCO$_3^-$	Glucose	Urea
Plasma	145	101	4 x 10^{-5}	24	4.5	6
Saliva	4	16	4 x 10^{-4}	3	0.05	5
Taste recognition threshold	(NaCl)		(HCl)	(NaHCO$_3$)	(Sucrose)	(Urea)
	12		0.8	10	30	90

*All concentrations are in mmol/l.

Bicarbonate
This is the most important buffering system in saliva but only at high flow rates, when it is an important buffer against acid produced by dental plaque. Its concentration varies from less than 1 mmol/l in unstimulated parotid saliva to almost 60 mmol/l at very high flow rates, with whole saliva elicited by chewing gum having a bicarbonate concentration of about 15 mmol/l. Thus, in unstimulated saliva, the level of bicarbonate ions is too low to be an effective buffer. This allows us to taste acid put into the mouth, since the resulting fall in pH can stimulate gustatory receptors. The bicarbonate in saliva though will facilitate the clearance of acid from the oesophagus in those with gastro-oesophageal reflux disease.

pH
Salivary pH is dependent on the bicarbonate concentration, an increase in which results in an increase in pH. The relationship between the pH and the bicarbonate concentration is given by the Henderson-Hasselbalch equation, pH = pK + log[HCO$_3^-$]/[H$_2$CO$_3$], in which the pK (about 6.1) and [H$_2$CO$_3$] (about 1.2 mmol/l) are virtually independent of the flow rate. The latter is in equilibrium with the pCO$_2$ which, in saliva, is about the same as that in venous blood. When the pH of saliva is to be measured, it is important to avoid exposure of the saliva to the atmosphere, as CO$_2$ will be released and the pH

Table 3.7 Calcium and inorganic phosphate concentrations in saliva

	Plasma saliva	Parotid saliva	SM* secretions	MMG**
Calcium (mmol/l)	2.5	0.9	2.0	2.1
Phosphate (mmol/l)	1.0	3.5	2.9	0.4
Flow rate#	–	1.2	1.2	–

* SM = submandibular saliva

** MMG = minor mucous gland

ml/min/gland pair

will be artificially elevated. At very low flow rates, the pH can be as low as 5.3, rising to 7.8 at very high parotid flow rates. Individuals with hyposalivation will thus have a low salivary pH and a low salivary buffering capacity because of the low bicarbonate concentration (Fig. 3.3).

Urea

The urea concentration in saliva (about 3–5 mmol/l) is only slightly lower than that in plasma. Urea can diffuse from saliva into dental plaque, where bacterial ureases convert it into carbon dioxide and ammonia, the latter causing an increase in pH. Computer simulation suggests that in the absence of salivary urea, the minimum pH of the Stephan curve (*see* Chapter 6) would be deeper by about 0.5 pH units. Patients with uraemia develop less caries, more calculus, and the resting pH of their plaque may be as high as 9.

Calcium and phosphate concentrations

Calcium and trivalent phosphate (PO_4^{3-}) ions, along with hydroxyl ions, maintain the saturation of saliva with respect to tooth mineral, and are therefore important in calculus formation and in protecting against the development of caries (*see* Chapter 8).

Saliva contains less calcium but more phosphate than does plasma (Table 3.7). The mechanisms responsible for a higher concentration of phosphate in saliva than in plasma are uncertain. In addition, secretions from different salivary glands have different concentrations of calcium and phosphate. For

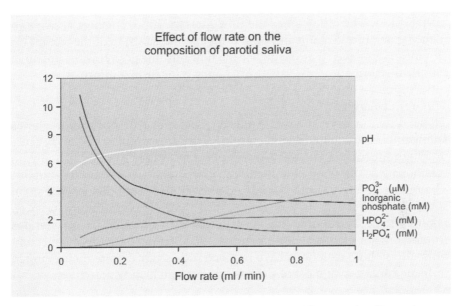

Fig. 3.5 The effect of salivary flow rate on the concentrations of the different species of inorganic phosphate in parotid saliva. Note that the PO_4^{3-} concentration is in μmol/l, whereas the concentrations of the other species are in mmol/l.

example, parotid saliva contains less calcium but more inorganic phosphate than does submandibular saliva, while the minor mucous gland secretions are very low in phosphate (Table 3.7).

A decreasing total phosphate concentration at high flow rates (Fig. 3.3) would seem to be bad for teeth, as it might result in undersaturation of the saliva with respect to tooth mineral. However, as the flow rate increases, so does the bicarbonate concentration and therefore the pH of saliva. A high pH alters the proportions of the four different phosphate species (H_3PO_4, $H_2PO_4^-$, HPO_4^{2-}, and PO_4^{3-}) such that there is a fall in $H_2PO_4^-$, a slight increase in HPO_4^{2-}, but a dramatic increase in PO_4^{3-}. It is the PO_4^{3-} which is the important ionic species with respect to the solubility of tooth mineral (*see* Chapter 8). Thus, although the total level of phosphate falls with increasing flow rate, the concentration of PO_4^{3-} actually increases (Fig. 3.5) as much as 40-fold when flow rate increases from the unstimulated level to high flow rates.

If, therefore, we consider the components of the ion product determining the solubility of tooth mineral, all three (Ca^{2+}, PO_4^{3-}, OH^-) increase with salivary flow. Thus the higher the flow rate, the more effective is saliva in reducing demineralization and promoting remineralization of the teeth. This also means, however, that the higher the flow rate, the greater is the potential for calculus formation to occur. (*See* Chapter 8 for further information.)

Minor mucous gland secretions

These differ in several ways from the secretions of the major glands (submandibular, sublingual and parotid). They are extremely viscous because of a high mucin content, very low in phosphate, they contain virtually no bicarbonate, so they have a low buffer capacity, and their pH is about neutrality. The main ions are sodium, potassium and chloride, and they are the main source of secretory IgA in the mouth. Their fluoride concentration has been reported to be several times higher than that in whole saliva or in secretions from the major glands. It is unfortunate that, mainly because of collection difficulties, these secretions have received little study despite their being in intimate contact with most of the oral mucosa and hard tissues.

Summary — clinical highlights

Salivary flow rate is nearly zero in sleep. Maximum cariogenic activity is likely to occur when people eat carbohydrate at night and then do not brush their teeth before going to sleep.

Dentists should be aware that many patients are taking medications (for example beta blockers) that have a tendency to reduce salivary flow, making the patient more susceptible to dental caries.

When salivary flow rate increases, this results in a higher salivary pH and bicarbonate content, which have beneficial effects on plaque pH if the stimulus to salivation does not include acid or additional sugar. The increased flow rate will itself help to remove carbohydrate from the mouth, and stir up the very thin film of saliva (*see* Chapter 5), which covers the oral surfaces. The bicarbonate will tend to diffuse into plaque and act as a buffer by neutralizing acids present in the plaque, allowing more time for remineralization of early caries.

Dentists should measure the unstimulated salivary flow rate of patients at appropriate intervals, as this would provide baseline values for future comparison. A very low salivary flow rate is an indication of caries susceptibility and influences the preventive treatment provided by the dentist.

Further reading

1 Dawes C. Rhythms in salivary flow rate and composition. *Internat J Chronobiol* 1972; **2**: 253–279.

2 Dawes C. How much saliva is enough for avoidance of xerostomia? *Caries Res* 2004; **38**: 236–240.

3 Dawes C. Physiological factors affecting salivary flow rate, oral sugar clearance, and the sensation of dry mouth in man. *J Dent Res* 1987; **66**: 648–653.

4 Mandel I D. The role of saliva in maintaining oral homeostasis. *J Am Dent Assoc* 1989; **119**: 298–304.

5 Nauntofte B, Tenovuo J O, Lagerlöf F. Secretion and composition of saliva. *In* Fejerskov O, Kidd E (Eds) *Dental Caries. The Disease and its Clinical Management.* pp 7–28. Oxford: Blackwell Munksgaard, 2003.

6 Simons D, Brailsford S R, Kidd E A M, Beighton D. The effect of medicated chewing gums on oral health in frail older people: a 1-year clinical trial. *J Am Geriatrics Soc* 2002; **50**: 1348–1353.

7 Watanabe S, Dawes C. The effects of different foods and concentrations of citric acid on the flow rate of whole saliva in man. *Arch Oral Biol* 1988; **33**: 1–5.

4

Xerostomia: aetiology, diagnosis, management and clinical implications

Jonathan A Ship

Introduction

Saliva plays a critical role in the preservation of oral-pharyngeal health. Complaints of a dry mouth (xerostomia) and diminished salivary output (salivary hypofunction) are common conditions, particularly in older populations. They can result in impaired food and beverage intake, a plethora of oral disorders, and diminished host defence and communication (Table 4.1). Persistent xerostomia and salivary hypofunction can produce significant and permanent oral and pharyngeal disorders and impair a person's quality of life.

Global estimates of xerostomia and salivary gland hypofunction are difficult to ascertain due to differences in study populations and diagnostic criteria, and limited sample sizes. Overall, the prevalence of xerostomia increases with age and affects ~30% of the population aged 65 years and older.

There are multiple causes of xerostomia and salivary hypofunction (Table 4.2), the most common being drug-induced xerostomia, since most older adults are taking at least one medication that causes salivary hypofunction. It is difficult, however, to estimate the true prevalence of xerostomia in older adults taking medications. The prevalence of xerostomia is nearly 100% among patients with Sjögren's syndrome, an autoimmune exocrinopathy affecting between 1–4% of older adults. Radiation of the head and neck for the treatment of cancer causes permanent xerostomia, which has a 100% prevalence rate if the dose is >25 Gy, but the numbers affected are relatively small compared with those older adults susceptible to medication-induced xerostomia. For example, in the USA, approximately 30,000 cases of head and neck cancers were diagnosed in 2003, and most of these patients required radiotherapy, which causes permanent salivary hypofunction and xerostomia. Estimates of the prevalence of xerostomia in adult ambulatory and nursing home populations range from 16–72%.[1] Combining the prevalence of xerostomia-associated conditions with the percentage of adults with these conditions who complain of xerostomia, yields the above-mentioned general estimate of approximately 30% xerostomia prevalence among adults 65 years and older.

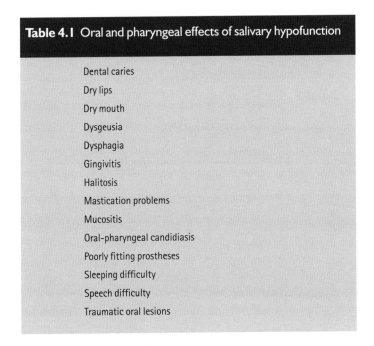

Table 4.1 Oral and pharyngeal effects of salivary hypofunction

Dental caries

Dry lips

Dry mouth

Dysgeusia

Dysphagia

Gingivitis

Halitosis

Mastication problems

Mucositis

Oral-pharyngeal candidiasis

Poorly fitting prostheses

Sleeping difficulty

Speech difficulty

Traumatic oral lesions

Aetiology of xerostomia and salivary hypofunction

Salivary gland pathology

Intra-oral sources of salivary gland pathology can be divided into three broad classifications: infectious, non-infectious and neoplastic (Table 4.3).[2] Bacterial infections are more common in older persons who experience salivary hypofunction secondary to medications, head and neck radiation, systemic diseases, or dehydration. Acute parotitis was commonly seen before the antibiotic era in terminally ill and dehydrated patients and contributed to mortality by sepsis. Now, acute parotitis is observed infrequently. Chronic parotitis is not unusual and it follows obstruction of a parotid duct with subsequent bacterial colonization and infection. Signs and symptoms of bacterial salivary infections include swelling, purulence from the major salivary gland duct and pain.

Viral infections occur in persons of all ages, particularly in immunocompromised patients, and preferentially involve parotid glands. Mumps is caused by paramyxovirus and presents as bilateral parotid gland

Table 4.2 Aetiology of xerostomia and salivary hypofunction

Condition	Examples
Medications	Anticholinergics, tricyclic antidepressants, sedatives, tranquilizers, antihistamines, antihypertensives, cytotoxic agents, anti-parkinsonian drugs, anti-seizure drugs, skeletal muscle relaxants
Oral diseases/conditions	Acute and chronic parotitis, sialolith, mucocele, partial/complete salivary obstruction
Systemic diseases/conditions	Mumps, Sjögren's syndrome, diabetes, HIV/AIDS, scleroderma, sarcoidosis, lupus, Alzheimer's disease, dehydration, graft-versus-host disease
Head and neck radiotherapy	

swellings in children. Cytomegalovirus infections tend to be mild with non-specific findings, and are observed primarily in adults.

Non-infectious (reactive) causes of salivary pathology are most commonly due to obstruction of a salivary gland excretory duct and can be divided into acute and chronic conditions. Acute salivary swellings usually result from an immediate partial or complete ductal obstruction (ie sialolithiasis), whereas chronic recurrent sialadenosis occurs as a result of prior infection and/or ductal scarring.

Mucoceles are the most common reactive lesion of the lower lip and are caused by local trauma. When a minor salivary gland duct is severed, mucin leaks into the surrounding connective tissue, resulting in a smooth-surfaced painless nodule in the submucosal tissues. Mucous cysts of the sublingual gland, and less frequently the submandibular gland, are referred to as ranulas. They present as either unilateral circumscribed lesions (subsequent to ductal obstruction and cystic dilation) or plunging lesions (following extravasation of saliva herniating through the tissues of the floor of the mouth and the mylohyoid muscle). Both types of ranulas require surgical excision and possible marsupialization of the cyst.

Most calculi (sialoliths, stones) develop in the submandibular duct system and are caused by calcification of mucous plugs and cellular debris, typically as a result of dehydration and glandular inactivity. Sialoliths occur infrequently in the parotid duct system and are considered rare in the sublingual and minor salivary glands.

Table 4.3 Classifications of intra-oral salivary gland pathologies

Pathology	Etiology
Infectious	
Acute sialadenitis	• Salivary hypofunction: secondary to dehydration, debilitation, medications
	• Bacterial species: *Staphylococcus aureus, S. pyogenes, Streptococcus pneumonia, E. coli*
Chronic recurrent sialadenitis	Bacterial species (see acute sialadenitis)
Viral sialadenitis	Paramyxovirus, cytomegalovirus
Non-infectious	
Sialectasis	Salivary hypofunction: secondary to dehydration and post-general anesthesia
Sialolithiasis	Salivary hypofunction: secondary to dehydration, debilitation, medications, metabolic disorders, poor oral hygiene
Sialadenosis	Malnutrition, alcoholic cirrhosis, diabetes mellitus, hyperlipidemia
Mucous cyst	Blockage of an excretory duct
Mucocele	Traumatic severance of a minor salivary gland duct, producing spillage of mucin into surrounding connective tissue
Neoplastic	
Benign tumours	Pleomorphic adenoma
	Monomorphic adenoma
Malignant tumours	Adenoid cystic carcinoma
	Mucoepidermoid carcinoma
	Acinic cell carcinoma
	Malignant mixed tumour[1]

[1]Carcinoma arising in a pleomorphic adenoma and squamous cell carcinoma

Most salivary gland tumours are benign, arising from epithelial tissues; however, neoplasms may originate from any adjacent tissue or structure (adipose, nerves, blood vessels, lymph nodes, lymphatics). The preponderance of benign salivary gland neoplasms occurs within the parotid gland, with the majority (80%) being pleomorphic adenomas. These tend to be unilateral and most commonly present as an asymptomatic mass in the tail of the parotid gland. They are slow growing, well delineated and encapsulated. Malignant salivary gland tumour incidence increases with age and these tumours are more common in the submandibular and sublingual glands, compared with the parotid gland. When epithelial neoplasms arise in the submandibular or sublingual glands, only 50% are benign.[3]

Mucoepidermoid carcinoma is the most common malignant salivary gland tumour, followed by adenoid cystic carcinoma (cylindroma), acinic cell carcinoma, adenocarcinoma and carcinoma arising in a pleomorphic adenoma. The most commonly affected intra-oral site is the palate followed by the upper lip. Adenoid cystic carcinomas are aggressive tumours that undergo perineural invasion. They have good 10-year survival rates but long-term mortality is likely. Signs and symptoms of a malignant salivary gland tumour include a swelling with facial nerve paralysis, pain or facial paresis.

Systemic diseases

There are numerous systemic conditions that have been associated with xerostomia and salivary hypofunction (Table 4.2), the most common being Sjögren's syndrome. Sjögren's syndrome is primarily a disease affecting women with a typical onset during the fourth or fifth decade of life.[4] Clinically, Sjögren's syndrome presents in either primary or secondary forms. Primary Sjögren's syndrome is characterized by xerostomia and xerophthalmia (dry eyes) which are the result of a progressive loss of salivary and lacrimal function. Secondary Sjögren's syndrome includes involvement of one or both of these exocrine sites in the presence of another connective tissue disease such as rheumatoid arthritis, systemic sclerosis or systemic lupus erythematosus. Lymphocytic infiltrates of salivary glands increase as the inflammatory disease progresses, ultimately producing acinar gland degeneration, necrosis, atrophy and complete destruction of the salivary gland parenchyma. Diagnosis requires a combination of objective salivary, lacrimal and serological criteria and subjective complaints of xerostomia or xerophthalmia.[5]

Other autoimmune conditions associated with Sjögren's syndrome and causing salivary hypofunction include rheumatoid arthritis, scleroderma and lupus. HIV+ infected individuals and those with AIDS frequently experience salivary hypofunction from lymphocytic destruction of the glands and as a sequela of medications. Diabetes may cause changes in salivary secretions and associations have been made between poor glycemic control, peripheral neuropathies and salivary hypofunction. Alzheimer's disease, Parkinson's disease, strokes, cystic fibrosis and dehydration will also inhibit salivary secretion.

It was previously thought that salivary function declined with greater age, yet it is now accepted that output from the major salivary glands does not undergo clinically significant decrements in healthy individuals.[6] There are reports of age-related decrements in several salivary constituents, whereas other studies report age-stable production of salivary electrolytes and proteins in the absence of major medical problems and medications. It is likely that numerous systemic diseases (eg Sjögren's syndrome) and their treatments (medications, head and neck radiation, chemotherapy) contribute significantly to salivary gland hypofunction in the elderly (Table 4.2).[7,8] It was recently demonstrated that the salivary glands of older persons are more vulnerable to the deleterious effects of medications compared with those of younger individuals,[9] confirming the finding of greater xerostomia prevalence among older adults, particularly those taking medications.

Medications

The most common cause of salivary hypofunction and xerostomia is prescription and non-prescription medications. For example, 80% of the most commonly prescribed medications have been reported to cause xerostomia,[10] with over 400 medications causing a side-effect of salivary gland hypofunction.[8] The intake of prescription medications increases with age with more than 75% of persons over the age of 65 years taking at least one prescription medication. Further, with the increased intake of prescription medications there is an increase in xerostomia.

The most common types of medications causing salivary hypofunction have anticholinergic effects, via inhibition of acetylcholine binding to muscarinic receptors on the acinar cells. This prevents initiation of the cascade of physiological events that ultimately result in water movement through acinar cells, into the ductal system, and ultimately into the mouth (*see* Chapter 2). Importantly, any drugs that inhibit neurotransmitter binding to acinar membrane receptors, or that interfere with ion transport pathways, may also adversely affect the quality and quantity of salivary output. These medications include tricyclic antidepressants, sedatives and tranquilizers, antihistamines, antihypertensives (alpha and beta blockers, diuretics, calcium channel blockers, angiotensin-converting enzyme inhibitors), cytotoxic agents, anti-parkinsonian, and anti-seizure drugs.[8]

Chemotherapy for cancer treatment has also been associated with salivary disorders. These changes appear to occur during and immediately after treatment. Most patients experience return of salivary function to pre-chemotherapy levels, yet long-term changes have been reported. Finally, radioactive iodine (I^{131}) used in treatment for cancers of the thyroid gland may cause parotid but not submandibular hypofunction in a dose-dependent fashion, since the salivary glands concentrate iodide to levels much higher than those in the blood.

Head and neck radiotherapy

Radiation therapy (RT), a common treatment modality for head and neck cancers, causes permanent salivary gland hypofunction and a persistent complaint of a dry mouth.[11] The serous acini of salivary glands are considered to be the most radiosensitive cells, followed by mucous acini. Experiments with rhesus monkeys suggest that irradiated serous salivary glands undergo interphase cell death by apoptosis. There is an increase in the intensity of degenerative changes with dose and time in serous acinar cells, which produces apoptosis at low doses and necrosis at high doses. Within one week of the start of irradiation (after 10 Gy have been delivered) salivary output declines by 60–90%, with later recovery only if the total dose to salivary tissue is <25 Gy.[12]

After the first week of RT, patients will experience viscous saliva, because serous cell loss results in diminished water secretion. Eventually, mucous cells are also affected, decreasing the overall volume of saliva produced.[11] As indicated above, there is a dose-dependent relationship between the amount of radiation delivered to oral tissues and the damage that eventually occurs. Importantly, thresholds of 23–25 Gy have been established above which permanent salivary gland destruction occurs, and below which salivary recovery can occur after the completion of radiotherapy.[12]

Diagnosis of xerostomia and salivary hypofunction

Subjective responses and questionnaires

The establishment of a diagnosis of xerostomia and salivary hypofunction is initiated with patients' complaints and can be advanced with the use of questionnaires (Table 4.4). Many of the common oral symptoms of dry mouth are associated with mealtime: altered taste, difficulty eating, chewing and swallowing, particularly dry foods, and especially without drinking accompanying liquids (Table 4.4). Patients complain of impaired denture retention, halitosis, stomatodynia and intolerance to acidic and spicy foods.[7] Night-time xerostomia is also common, since salivary output normally reaches its lowest circadian level during sleep and may be exacerbated by mouth-breathing.[13]

Table 4.4 Subjective measures of xerostomia

Measure	Response	Reference
Do you have difficulties swallowing any foods?	Yes/no	[14]
Does your mouth feel dry when eating a meal?	Yes/no	[14]
Do you sip liquids to aid in swallowing dry foods?	Yes/no	[14]
Does the amount of saliva in your mouth seem to be too little, too much or you don't notice it?	Yes/no	[14]
Rate the difficulty you experience in speaking due to dryness	0–10 scale[1]	[16]
Rate the difficulty you experience in swallowing due to dryness	0–10 scale[1]	[16]
Rate how much saliva is in your mouth	0–10 scale[2]	[16]
Rate the dryness of your mouth	0–10 scale[3]	[16]
Rate the dryness of your throat	0–10 scale[3]	[16]
Rate the dryness of your lips	0–10 scale[3]	[16]
Rate the dryness of your tongue	0–10 scale[3]	[16]
Rate the level of your thirst	0–10 scale[4]	[16]
Dryness of lips	Present/absent	[15]
Dryness of buccal mucosa	Present/absent	[15]
I sip liquids to aid in swallowing food	1–5 scale[5]	[17]
My mouth feels dry when eating a meal	1–5 scale[5]	[17]
I get up at night to drink	1–5 scale[5]	[17]
I have difficulty in eating dry foods	1–5 scale[5]	[17]
I suck sweets or cough lollies to relieve dry mouth	1–5 scale[5]	[17]
I have difficulties swallowing certain foods	1–5 scale[5]	[17]
I have a burning sensation in my gums	1–5 scale[5]	[17]
I have a burning sensation in my tongue	1–5 scale[5]	[17]
My gums itch	1–5 scale[5]	[17]
My tongue itches	1–5 scale[5]	[17]
The skin of my face feels dry	1–5 scale[5]	[17]
My eyes feel dry	1–5 scale[5]	[17]
My lips feel dry	1–5 scale[5]	[17]
The inside of my nose feels dry	1–5 scale[5]	[17]

[1]From 'Not difficult at all' to 'Very difficult'; [2]From 'A lot' to 'None'; [3]From 'Not dry at all' to 'Very dry'; [4]From 'Not thirsty at all' to 'Very thirsty'; [5]1 = 'never', 2 = 'hardly ever', 3 = 'occasionally', 4 = 'fairly often', 5 = 'very

Several investigations have examined the utility and reliability of using standardized questionnaires for diagnosis of salivary hypofunction.[14–17] Querying a person about nocturnal or early morning xerostomia is less reliable for establishing a diagnosis of salivary hypofunction since salivary flow rate is very low during sleep (*see* Chapter 3) and mouth-breathing can dehydrate the oral mucosal tissues. An interesting finding is that in persons who report having a very dry mouth, the residual volume of saliva is approximately 70% of normal. These data suggest that xerostomia may be due, in part, to localized areas of dryness in the mouth (eg the anterior portion of the hard palate), rather than to generalized whole mouth dryness.

General oral examination
Extra-oral findings of salivary hypofunction include dry and cracked lips that are frequently colonized with *Candida* species (angular cheilitis). Visible and palpable enlarged major salivary glands occur secondary to salivary infections and obstructions (eg bacterial parotitis, mumps, Sjögren's syndrome). A swollen parotid gland can displace the earlobe and extend inferiorly over the angle of the mandible, whereas an enlarged submandibular gland is palpated medial to the posterior–inferior border of the mandible.

There are numerous intra-oral indications of salivary hypofunction. Oral mucosal surfaces become desiccated and easily friable. The tongue can lose its filiform papillae and will appear dry, erythemic and raw with an irritated dorsal surface. Mucosal tissues are susceptible to developing microbial infections, the most common being candidiasis. This intra-oral fungal infection manifests itself as erythematous candidiasis beneath prostheses and as pseudo-membranous candidiasis, which produces a white plaque that can be removed from mucosal surfaces. Clinicians can also observe decreased or absent saliva pooling in the anterior floor of the mouth.

A second frequent problem is dental caries, which occurs both on coronal and root surfaces. New caries lesions can develop on surfaces not normally affected (eg incisal edges of anterior teeth) and recurrent lesions are prevalent on the margins of existing restorations.

Edentulous and partially edentulous adults using removable prostheses have diminished denture retention, which will impact adversely on chewing, swallowing, speech and nutritional intake. Denture-bearing tissues can develop erythematous candidiasis and traumatic and painful lesions due to tissue trauma.

Saliva collection

Numerous investigators have attempted to define the lower limits of 'normal' salivary flow rates. However, there is substantial variability in flow rates that makes it difficult to define diagnostically useful ranges of glandular fluid production (*see* Chapter 3). In studies of healthy persons across the lifespan, unstimulated fluid secretion varies 10–100-fold, while stimulated secretion varies 10–20-fold.[18]

In patients considered to be at risk for developing salivary hypofunction, it would be useful to monitor salivary flow rates over time. Most investigators consider a diagnosis of salivary hypofunction if the unstimulated whole salivary flow rate is less than 0.1 ml/min using standardized techniques. Unstimulated secretions are probably more indicative of dry mouth complaints compared with stimulated secretions, since saliva is produced under unstimulated conditions the vast majority of hours a person is awake. The most common collection technique for unstimulated whole saliva is to have a patient refrain from eating, drinking, smoking or performing oral hygiene for at least 60 minutes prior to saliva collection. The patient is seated in a quiet environment with their head tilted forward. Immediately before the test begins they should swallow any residual saliva that may be in their mouth. The time is recorded and the person is instructed to allow saliva to flow gently into a pre-weighed test tube or other container placed under their chin for five minutes without swallowing or spitting. At five minutes the person in instructed to expectorate the remaining saliva from their mouth into the container. The volume is recorded gravimetrically, and expressed as ml/min.

Stimulated whole salivary flow rates less than 0.5 ml/min are also considered to be suggestive of salivary hypofunction. The most common technique for collecting this form of saliva is with the use of a standard piece of paraffin wax or unflavoured gum base (typically 1–2 g). A test tube or similar container with the paraffin or gum base is weighed prior to saliva collection. The person is instructed to swallow any residual saliva that may be in their mouth before the saliva collection begins. A timer begins and the person is instructed to chew the wax or gum base at a rate of 60 chews/minute (1 chew/second). Without swallowing, they expectorate all saliva in their mouth into the pre-weighed container placed under their chin at each 60-second interval. At five minutes the person is instructed to expectorate the remaining saliva and wax from their mouth into the container and the collection is completed. The volume is recorded gravimetrically, and expressed as ml/min.

Recent research data suggest that values below 45% of normal levels can be used to define salivary hypofunction.[19] It is also generally accepted that when an individual's glandular fluid production is decreased by about 50%, they will begin to experience symptoms of oral dryness.[20] The best strategy is simply to monitor a patient's salivary health (both objectively and subjectively) over time to determine whether there are demonstrable changes.[18]

Histopathology

The treatment of lesions and tumours associated with the salivary glands starts with an appropriate diagnosis and frequently this includes examination of histopathological tissue. Incisional or excisional biopsies and histopathological evaluation are critically important. For Sjögren's syndrome, minor salivary glands are biopsied to examine for a focal lymphocytic sialadenitis. A focus score ≥1 is used as part of the objective criteria in the Revised European Classification Criteria for Sjögren's syndrome.[5] A focus score is defined as the number of lymphocytic foci which are adjacent to normal-appearing mucous acini and contain >50 lymphocytes per 4 mm^2 of glandular tissue.[21]

Imaging

Sialograms can identify changes in the salivary gland architecture and are performed with radio-opaque iodine and extra-oral radiographs (lateral cephalograms, panographs, etc.). Radioactive isotope scintiscans (eg Tc^{99} pertechnetate) can provide a qualitative functional assessment of the major salivary glands. Decreased uptake of radio-isotopes and delayed expulsion are associated with salivary hypofunction. MRI and CT scans will help rule out salivary gland tumours and other pathoses associated with the craniofacial region that may adversely affect salivation.

Serology

Serological studies are critically important for the diagnosis of Sjögren's syndrome. Autoantibodies (particularly anti-Ro/SSA, anti-La/SSB and rheumatoid factor) are frequently present in Sjögren's syndrome and tend to be higher in family members than in the general population.[5] Caucasian patients with primary Sjögren's syndrome also often have the HLA-DR3 and HLA-DQ2 alleles. Other serological factors, such as an elevated erythrocyte sedimentation rate and antinuclear antibody (ANA) levels greater than 1:160, tend to be positive in patients with autoimmune diseases who may have secondary Sjögren's syndrome. Abnormal levels of anti-SM and anti-RNP are suggestive of systemic lupus erythematosus, while Scl-70 can be positive in progressive systemic sclerosis (scleroderma).

Clinical implications of xerostomia and salivary hypofunction

Dental caries and dental erosion

One of the most common oral conditions that develop as a result of salivary hypofunction is new and recurrent dental caries. In the presence of persistent salivary hypofunction, the inability of the salivary system to restore oral pH towards neutrality and inhibit certain bacteria after food and beverage ingestion leads to an oral environment conducive to microbial colonization with caries-associated microorganisms and enamel demineralization. The margins of existing restorations are also vulnerable to recurrent decay. Salivary hypofunction-associated root surface caries is a particularly difficult condition to diagnose and treat and therefore identification of patients at risk will allow measures to be taken to preserve the dentition.

Insufficient saliva enhances the erosion of tooth surfaces by chemical dissolution when the oral pH remains excessively acidic. With deficient remineralization, dental abrasion and attrition are a more frequent occurrence in patients with salivary hypofunction. The cervical regions of teeth occasionally receive greater abrasion from toothbrushes and are susceptible to dental erosion. Occlusal and incisal surfaces exposed to attritional and traumatic forces can also undergo greater loss of enamel and dentine when there is insufficient saliva to permit remineralization.

Gingivitis

The increase in salivary output during and immediately after the consumption of foods and fluids assists in the lavage of the oral cavity and the removal of food particles from oral surfaces. Conversely, salivary hypofunction is frequently associated with retained food particles, particularly in interproximal regions and beneath denture surfaces, and can cause gingivitis. Long-standing gingivitis can develop into periodontal loss of attachment, so patients with chronic hyposalivation are at risk for developing gingival and periodontal problems.

Interestingly, most studies have not demonstrated significantly greater levels of periodontal disease in patients with Sjögren's syndrome compared with healthy controls,[22] which may be due to greater attention to oral health and more frequent use of professional dental services. In addition, while several studies have demonstrated significantly greater numbers of caries-associated mutans streptococci and lactobacilli in patients with salivary hypofunction compared with healthy controls, similar levels of microorganisms associated with gingival inflammation were detected in both populations.[23] Therefore, the primary dental problem in patients with salivary hypofunction is dental caries, with less risk (but greater than that for healthy individuals) for developing gingival and periodontal disorders.

Impaired use of removable prostheses

Removable prostheses depend upon a thin film of saliva on mucosal surfaces in order to enhance adhesion. Accordingly, changes in saliva quantity and quality have been associated with impaired use of dental prostheses. Most commonly, salivary hypofunction leads to trauma to the desiccated, friable tissues and an increased rate of oral microbial infections. Hyposalivation patients using removable prostheses frequently require denture adhesives to assist in retention of their appliances.

Oral fungal infections

Decreased salivary output leads to oral mucositis, pain and increased susceptibility to developing microbial infections, the most prevalent of which is candidiasis. This fungal infection is caused by *Candida albicans*, a commensal organism that normally resides in the oral cavity. There are five clinical manifestations of oral candidiasis: angular cheilitis of the lips, erythematous candidiasis (denture stomatitis), atrophic candidiasis, hyperplastic candidiasis and pseudomembraneous candidiasis.

Dysgeusia

Saliva plays a critically important role in taste function as a solvent for food, a carrier of taste-eliciting molecules and through its composition (*see* Chapter 3). Accordingly, when salivary output is reduced, taste function can be adversely affected (dysgeusia).[24] Head and neck radiation has deleterious effects on both taste cells and salivary glands and thus directly and indirectly affects gustation. Other diseases and medical problems adversely affect the composition of saliva (eg adrenergic blocking agents), which could influence taste. While no specific salivary constituent has been directly connected to gustatory disorders, it has

Library
Knowledge Spa
Royal Cornwall Hospital
Treliske
Truro. TR1 3HD

Xerostomia

been hypothesized that certain salivary electrolytes and minerals contribute to normal taste sensation.

Dysphagia

Salivary hypofunction also contributes to difficulty with chewing and swallowing (dysphagia). Swallowing occurs in three stages: oral, pharyngeal and oesophageal. Each stage requires adequate lubrication of mucosal tissues to ensure a safe and efficient swallow. It requires greater time to perform a single as well as repeated multiple swallowing movements in subjects with salivary hypofunction. Therefore, dysphagia is more prevalent among patients with salivary hypofunction. Importantly, dysphagia is a significant risk for developing aspiration pneumonia, a condition which carries great morbidity and mortality, particularly in those inhabiting long-term care institutions.

Impaired quality of life

Many of the oral-pharyngeal sequelae of salivary hypofunction and the chronic complaints of a dry mouth lead to an impaired quality of life. Dento-alveolar and oropharyngeal infections can rapidly lead to systemic disease, particularly in medically compromised patients. Desiccated and friable oral mucosal tissues are more likely to develop traumatic lesions, especially in denture-wearing adults, which cause pain and interfere with nutritional intake. Also, dysgeusia, dysphagia and difficulty chewing food secondary to salivary hypofunction can lead to changes in food and fluid selection that compromise nutritional status. The speech and eating difficulties that develop can impair social interactions and may cause some patients to avoid social engagements. Dysphagia increases susceptibility to aspiration pneumonia and colonization of the lungs with Gram-negative anaerobes from the gingival sulcus.[25]

Management of xerostomia and salivary dysfunction

Overview

The initial step in the management of xerostomia is the establishment of a diagnosis. This frequently involves a multidisciplinary team of health care practitioners where communication is critical since many patients have concomitant medical problems and the frequent complications of polypharmacy. The second step is scheduling frequent dental evaluations due to the high prevalence of oral complications.[7] Maintenance of proper oral hygiene and hydration (water is the drink of choice) are helpful. Several habits, such as smoking, mouth-breathing and consumption of caffeine-containing beverages, have been shown to increase the risk of xerostomia. Limiting or stopping these practices should lessen the severity of dry mouth symptoms. A low-sugar diet, daily topical fluoride use (eg fluoride toothpaste and mouthrinses), antimicrobial mouthrinses and use of sugar-free gum to stimulate salivary flow, help to prevent dental caries.

There are many biomaterials available for the restoration of dental caries and glass-ionomer resins and liners are well suited for patients with salivary hypofunction who are caries-susceptible. These materials provide sustained fluoride release that reduces the incidence of recurrent caries and the fluoride is considered 'rechargeable' when the patient uses a fluoridated rinse or toothpaste.

Dry mucosal surfaces and dysphagia are managed with oral moisturizers, lubricants and artificial salivas, as well as careful use of fluids during eating. The night time use of bedside humidifiers can assist nocturnal xerostomia.

Patients must be instructed on the frequent use of fluids during eating, particularly for dry and rough foods. Eating and swallowing problems secondary to salivary hypofunction can impair intake of fibre-rich foods, restricting some adults to a primarily soft and carbohydrate diet. Accordingly, patients must be counselled on a well-balanced, nutritionally adequate diet and the importance of limiting sugar intake, particularly between meals.

Gustatory and masticatory stimulation
If there are remaining viable salivary glands, stimulation techniques using sugar-free chewing gum, candies (sweets) and mints can stimulate salivary output. Chewing sugarless gum is an extremely effective and continuous sialogogue, since it increases salivary output and increases salivary pH and buffer capacity. Citric acid, which is present in fruits as well as sour and sugarless candies or lozenges, may also be used to stimulate salivary output. However, dentate individuals should refrain from excessive use of acid-containing substances, since they could cause dental erosion.

Pharmacological stimulation
Treating xerostomia with medications that enhance salivation is another therapeutic option, particularly in the relatively healthy person for whom polypharmacy may not be a critical concern. Secretagogues such as pilocarpine

(a non-specific muscarinic agonist) can increase secretion rates and diminish xerostomic complaints in patients with sufficient remaining exocrine tissue.[26] Pilocarpine has been approved by the US Food and Drug Administration (FDA) for the treatment of xerostomia and salivary hypofunction in patients with Sjögren's syndrome as well as in patients who have received head and neck radiotherapy for cancer. Pilocarpine is typically given in a dosage of 5 mg orally three times a day and before bedtime. When taken approximately 30 minutes before mealtime, patients may benefit from the increased salivation in eating their meal. The total daily dose should not exceed 30 mg. Adverse effects include increased perspiration, greater bowel and bladder motility, and feeling hot and flushed. Patients with a history of bronchospasm, uncontrolled asthma, severe chronic obstructive pulmonary disease, congestive heart disease and angle closure glaucoma should not take pilocarpine.

Another pharmacological sialogogue is cevimeline, which has FDA approval for the treatment of dry mouth in Sjögren's syndrome in a dosage of 30 mg orally three times daily. Like pilocarpine, it is a muscarinic agonist that increases production of saliva. Pilocarpine is a non-selective muscarinic agonist, whereas cevimeline reportedly has a higher affinity for M1 and M3 muscarinic receptor subtypes. Since M2 and M4 receptors are located on cardiac and lung tissues, cevimeline can enhance salivary secretions while minimizing adverse effects on pulmonary and cardiac function. Patients with uncontrolled asthma, significant cardiac disease and angle closure glaucoma should not take cevimeline.

Drug substitution and deletion

Instead of prescribing xerostomia-associated drugs, substitution with similar types of medications with fewer xerostomic side-effects is preferred. For example, serotonin-specific reuptake inhibitors (SSRIs) have been reported to cause less dry mouth than tricyclic antidepressants. If anticholinergic medications can be taken during the daytime, nocturnal xerostomia can be diminished since salivary output is lowest at night. Furthermore, if drug dosages can be divided, unwanted side-effects from a large single dose can be avoided. Scrutiny of drug side-effects (see www.drymouth.info) can assist in diminishing the xerostomic potential of many pharmaceuticals used by patients presenting with xerostomia.

Polypharmacy is a common problem among the elderly, who can be treated concomitantly by multiple health care providers. Occasionally, medications with xerostomic sequelae may no longer be required, but the patient continues to take them. Other times multiple drugs are prescribed for similar medical conditions by different health care providers. Under these conditions it is advisable to recommend critical review of all medications. Perhaps some can be substituted or even deleted from the daily regimen to diminish unwanted side-effects including xerostomia and salivary hypofunction.

Salivary replacements

Artificial saliva and lubricants may ameliorate some xerostomic symptoms in patients who have remaining salivary tissue as well as those who have no viable salivary glands. These products tend to diminish the sensation of oral dryness and improve oral functioning. The choice of product depends on effect duration, lubrication, taste, delivery system and cost; many patients nevertheless primarily use water.[27] Several products currently available without a prescription include Biotene (mouthwash, toothpaste and chewing gum), Saliva Orthana (a mucin-based artificial saliva), Freedent (a low-tack, sugar-free chewing gum) and Oralbalance gel.

Acupuncture

Over the last decade there has been some interest in using acupuncture techniques to enhance salivation.[28] There are data suggesting that acupuncture therapy can increase the flow rate of stimulated saliva for up to six months after the completion of radiotherapy.[28] Although this treatment modality is not commonly utilized, it presents an option for patients who respond well to muscarinic agonists (eg pilocarpine, cevimeline) yet have difficulty taking these medications due to secondary side-effects.

Salivary gland sparing radiotherapy

Three-dimensional treatment planning and dose delivery techniques have been devised to limit radiation exposure to salivary glands in an attempt to preserve salivary function after radiotherapy. Significant dose reductions have been achieved to parotid glands on the contralateral side of the primary tumour, resulting in retention of secretory ability, reduction of xerostomia and improvement of xerostomia-related quality of life.[29]

Further, it appears that reducing the dose to the salivary glands does not impair radiation efficacy with respect to tumours and lymph nodes considered to be at risk for cancer spread, and that long-term survival may not be reduced with these radiation-sparing techniques.

Cytoprotectants

A new category of drugs has been developed that may protect oral mucosal and salivary gland tissues during chemotherapy and head and neck radiotherapy. The most commonly used is Amifostine, a broad-spectrum cyto- and radio-protectant, which provides mucosal and organ protection against myelotoxicity, nephrotoxicity, mucositis and xerostomia associated with various chemotherapy and radiation modalities. Specifically, Amifostine has received FDA approval for reduction of xerostomia in patients receiving head and neck radiotherapy[30] and it has also demonstrated efficacy in reducing mucositis and candidiasis in these patients. Amifostine is given intravenously (200 mg/m^2) or subcutaneously (500 mg) 30–60 minutes prior to each dose of external beam RT. Common side-effects include hypotension, nausea and vomiting. Accordingly, fluids and anti-nausea medications are required daily to prevent serious side-effects.

Salivary gland surgical transfer

Surgical techniques have been used to spare salivary glands from head and neck radiotherapy. One technique involves transferring the contralateral submandibular gland to the submental region, which can shield the gland from the damage induced by external beam radiation.[31] Post-radiotherapy follow up data suggest fewer complaints of xerostomia with few surgical complications. Therefore this and other surgical techniques could be combined with chemotherapeutic agents to spare salivary glands from toxicity and stimulate existing secretions to compensate for radiotherapy-destroyed glands.

Gene therapy

New research in the field of gene therapy may make it possible to prevent damage to, as well as correct, already damaged salivary glands.[32] Transfer of genes to salivary glands has already been demonstrated using viral and non-viral vectors in animal models. The close access to salivary gland cells via the intra-oral cannulation of the main excretory ducts permits relatively non-invasive delivery of vectors and transferring genes. With increased pathobiological understanding and biotechnological improvements, it is believed that gene transfer may become a common modality for treating certain salivary gland disorders in the future.[32]

Clinical highlights

1. The prevalence of xerostomia increases with age and affects ~30% of the population aged 65 years and older.

2. There are multiple causes of xerostomia and salivary hypofunction, the most common being drugs with anticholinergic side-effects, Sjogren's syndrome, and head and neck radiotherapy for the treatment of cancer.

3. There are multiple intra-oral causes of salivary gland pathology and they are divided into three classifications: infectious (bacterial and viral), non-infectious (obstructions) and neoplastic.

4. Many of the common oral symptoms of dry mouth are associated with mealtime: altered taste, difficulty eating, chewing and swallowing, particularly dry foods, and especially without drinking accompanying liquids.

5. Diagnostic methods for salivary disorders include a thorough head, neck and oral examination, collection of saliva, histopathological examination of biopsy specimens, serology, cultures and imaging studies.

6. The most frequent adverse oral consequences of salivary hypofunction are dental caries, gingivitis, oral fungal infections, impaired prosthesis retention, dysphagia and dysgeusia.

7. Treating salivary hypofunction if there are remaining viable salivary glands requires stimulation techniques, such as using sugar-free chewing gum, candies (sweets) and mints, and the use of systemically administered cholinergic agonist medications (pilocarpine hydrochloride and cevimeline hydrochloride).

8. Techniques to treat drug-induced xerostomia include drug substitution (exchanging one xerostomia-causing drug with a similar type of medication with fewer side-effects) and deletion of unnecessary drugs that are causing polypharmacy-induced xerostomia.

9. Artificial saliva and lubricants may ameliorate some xerostomic symptoms and improve oral function in patients who have remaining salivary tissue as well as those who have no viable salivary glands.

References

1 Thomson W M, Chalmers J M, Spencer A J, Ketabi M. The occurrence of xerostomia and salivary gland hypofunction in a population-based sample of older South Australians. Spec Care Dent 1999; 19 : 20–23.

2 Norman J E, Mitchell R D. Unusual conditions of the major and minor salivary glands. Int J Oral Maxofac Surg 1998; 27: 157–172.

3 Nagler R M, Laufer D. Tumors of the major and minor salivary glands: review of 25 years of experience. Anticancer Res 1997; 17: 701–707.

4 Fox R I, Stern M, Michelson P. Update in Sjogren syndrome. Curr Opin Rheum 2000; 12: 391–398.

5 Vitali C, Bombardieri S, Jonsson R, Moutsopoulos H M, Alexander EL, Carsons S E, et al. Classification criteria for Sjogren's syndrome: a revised version of the European criteria proposed by the American-European Consensus Group. Ann Rheum Dis 2002; 61: 554–558.

6 Ship J A, Nolan N, Puckett S. Longitudinal analysis of parotid and submandibular salivary flow rates in healthy, different-aged adults. J Gerontol Med Sci 1995; 50A: M285–M289.

7 Atkinson J C, Wu A. Salivary gland dysfunction: causes, symptoms, treatment. J Amer Dent Assoc 1994; 125: 409–416.

8 Sreebny L M, Schwartz S S. A reference guide to drugs and dry mouth—2nd edition. Gerodontology 1997; 14: 33–47.

9 Ghezzi E M, Ship J A. Aging and secretory reserve capacity of major salivary glands. J Dent Res 2003; 82: 844–848.

10 Smith R G, Burtner A P. Oral side-effects of the most frequently prescribed drugs. Spec Care Dent 1994; 14: 96–102.

11 Henson B S, Eisbruch A, D'Hondt E, Ship J A. Two-year longitudinal study of parotid salivary flow rates in head and neck cancer patients receiving unilateral neck parotid-sparing radiotherapy treatment. Oral Oncol 1999; 35: 234–241.

12 Eisbruch A, Ten Haken R K, Kim H M, Marsh L H, Ship J A. Dose, volume, and function relationships in parotid salivary glands following conformal and intensity modulated irradiation of head and neck cancer. Int J Rad Oncol Biol Phys 1999; 45: 577–587.

13 Dawes C. Circadian rhythms in the flow rate and composition of unstimulated and stimulated human submandibular saliva. J Physiol 1975; 244: 535–548.

14 Fox P C, Busch K A, Baum B J. Subjective reports of xerostomia and objective measures of salivary gland performance. J Amer Dent Assoc 1987; 115: 581–584.

15 Navazesh M, Christensen C, Brightman V. Clinical criteria for the diagnosis of salivary gland hypofunction. J Dent Res 1992; 71: 1363–1369.

16 Pai S, Ghezzi E M, Ship J A. Development of a Visual Analogue Scale questionnaire for subjective assessment of salivary dysfunction. Oral Surg Oral Med Oral Path Oral Radiol Endo 2001; 91: 311–316.

17 Thomson W M, Chalmers J M, Spencer A J, Williams S M. The Xerostomia Inventory: a multi-item approach to measuring dry mouth. Comm Dent Health 1999; 16: 12–17.

18 Ship J A, Fox P C, Baum B J. How much saliva is enough? Normal function defined. J Amer Dent Assoc 1991; 122: 63–69.

19 Ghezzi E M, Lange L A, Ship J A. Determination of variation of stimulated salivary flow rates. J Dent Res 2000; 79: 1874–1878.

20 Dawes C. Physiological factors affecting salivary flow rate, oral sugar clearance, and the sensation of dry mouth in man. J Dent Res 1987; 66 (Spec Issue): 648–653.

21 Daniels T E, Whitcher J P. Association of patterns of labial salivary gland inflammation with keratoconjunctivitis sicca. Analysis of 618 patients with suspected Sjogren's syndrome. Arthritis Rheum 1994; 37: 869–877.

22 Jorkjend L, Johansson A, Johansson A K, Bergenholtz A. Periodontitis, caries and salivary factors in Sjogren's syndrome patients compared to sex- and age-matched controls. J Oral Rehab 2003; 30: 369–378.

23 Almstahl A, Wikstrom M. Oral microflora in subjects with reduced salivary secretion. J Dent Res 1999; 78: 1410–1416.

24 Spielman A I. Interaction of saliva and taste. J Dent Res 1990; 69: 838–843.

25 Loesche W J, Schork A, Terpenning M S, Chen Y M, Stoll J. Factors which influence levels of selected organisms in saliva of older individuals. J Clin Micro 1995; 33: 2550–2557.

26 Vivino F B, Al-Hashimi I, Khan Z, LeVeque F G, Salisbury P L 3rd, Tran-Johnson T K, et al. Pilocarpine tablets for the treatment of dry mouth and dry eye symptoms in patients with Sjogren syndrome: a randomized, placebo-controlled, fixed-dose, multicenter trial. P92-01 Study Group. Arch Int Med 1999; 159: 174–181.

27 Epstein J B, Stevenson-Moore P. A clinical comparative trial of saliva substitutes in radiation-induced salivary gland hypofunction. *Spec Care Dent* 1992; **12**: 21–23.
28 Blom M, Lundeberg T. Long-term follow-up of patients treated with acupuncture for xerostomia and the influence of additional treatment. *Oral Dis* 2000; **6**: 15–24.
29 Malouf J G, Aragon C, Henson B S, Eisbruch A, Ship J A. Influence of parotid-sparing radiotherapy on xerostomia in head and neck cancer patients. *Cancer Detect Prev* 2003; **27**: 305–310.
30 Brizel D M, Wasserman T H, Henke M, Stmad V, Rudat V, Monnier A, *et al*. Phase III randomized trial of amifostine as a radioprotector in head and neck cancer. *J Clin Oncol* 2000; **18**: 3339–3345. Erratum in *J Clin Oncol* 2000; **18**: 4110–4111.
31 Jha N, Seikaly H, Harris J, Williams D, Liu R, McGaw T, *et al*. Prevention of radiation induced xerostomia by surgical transfer of submandibular salivary gland into the submental space. *Radiother Oncol* 2003; **66**: 283–289.
32 Baum B J, Goldsmith C M, Hoque A T, Wellner R B, Baccaglini L, Ding C, *et al*. Salivary glands as a model for craniofacial applications of gene transfer. *Int J Oral Max Surg* 2000; **29**: 163–166.

Salivary clearance and its effects on oral health

C Dawes

5

Differences in the rates of salivary clearance of carbohydrates from food, acids from plaque, and therapeutic substances (for example fluoride) help to explain differences in disease susceptibility among individuals and at various sites within a single mouth.

A large number of substances pass through the oral cavity every day, some of which, such as sucrose or acids, are a threat to the health of the mouth, with its unique and vulnerable tissues. Other substances, such as fluoride, may act as a defence, promoting oral health.

Many substances will dissolve in saliva, from which they may then diffuse into, or react with, the oral tissues. The effect of incoming freshly secreted saliva, together with the swallowing process, is to reduce the concentration of exogenous substances, a process that is described as salivary clearance.

Thus, a rapid salivary clearance of harmful substances is beneficial for oral health, while the reverse is true for protective substances.

Models of salivary clearance

The SwenanderLanke model

The first model of salivary clearance was a simple one suggested by Swenander-Lanke in the mid-1940s.[1] In her model, a chemical – sucrose – dissolves in saliva (of volume V) to create an initial concentration (C_0). Saliva flows at a constant rate (F) into the mouth and is continuously removed (swallowed) at the same rate. The sucrose concentration (C_t) at a later time (t) can be shown to be given by $C_t = C_0.e^{-Ft/V}$. In experimental studies, a graph of the logarithm of the sucrose concentration versus time usually forms a straight line, but only if the plot is begun after the salivary flow rate has returned to the unstimulated rate following its initial rise due to the gustatory stimulation. The rate of decrease in concentration can also be described by using the time taken for the sucrose concentration to decrease by half, or the time taken for the concentration to fall to a given low level.

The Dawes model

A more recent model describes the swallowing process as being equivalent to the action of an incomplete siphon (Fig. 5.1).[2] After a swallow, the mouth retains a minimum volume of saliva, called the residual volume. Saliva then flows into the mouth at a rate dependent initially on the stimulating effect of the ingested substance but later, once the concentration is below the taste threshold, or after taste adaptation has occurred, on the unstimulated flow rate. The volume of saliva in the mouth thus increases until a maximum volume is reached. This stimulates the subject to swallow, which clears some of the substance from the oral cavity. The remainder (dissolved in the residual volume of saliva) is then progressively diluted by more saliva entering the mouth until the maximum volume is reached again, and another swallow occurs. The Dawes model has been used to describe with considerable accuracy the clearance of substances, including sucrose, which do not bind to oral surfaces.

Other studies have indicated that with some substances, clearance may occur in two stages, rapidly from the bulk of the saliva, and more slowly from stagnation areas.

Clearance of substances with binding properties

Fluoride

For fluoride, which is a natural component of saliva, and which reacts with the teeth and with plaque, the Dawes model requires further refinement, since plaque fluoride levels can be elevated for several hours following a fluoride rinse or intake of a fluoride tablet and can constitute a 'reservoir' of fluoride.[3]

During the early phase of clearance, when the salivary concentration is still high, some of the fluoride will diffuse into dental plaque, or bind to the oral mucosa, from which it is later redistributed back into the bulk saliva. This will delay clearance of fluoride, as will the formation of calcium fluoride deposits on the teeth. These can be formed at higher fluoride concentrations and they will later dissolve slowly. Also, most of the fluoride that is swallowed will be absorbed from the gastrointestinal tract into the blood and then a very small fraction of this (<0.2%) will be recycled via the salivary glands. When all of these factors are built into a computer model, it is possible to evaluate the effects of a single variable on clearance while keeping other variables constant.[4]

72

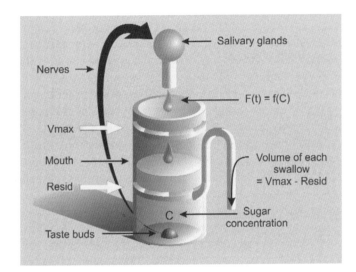

Fig. 5.1 The Dawes (1983) model of oral clearance. Saliva is produced at a rate dependent on the concentration of sugar in the saliva. When a maximum volume of saliva (Vmax) is reached, a swallow occurs and the salivary volume decreases to a residual volume (Resid), thereby eliminating some of the sugar.

Labels in figure: Salivary glands; Nerves →; $F(t) = f(C)$; Vmax; Mouth; Volume of each swallow = Vmax - Resid; Resid; C; Sugar concentration; Taste buds

Chlorhexidine

Chlorhexidine, in the form of rinses, gels or varnishes, is an antibacterial agent used for plaque control and for the prevention of both dental caries and periodontitis. An important property (termed substantivity) of chlorhexidine is its ability to bind more strongly than other antibacterial substances to the oral surfaces. This greatly delays its clearance from the mouth, thereby prolonging its effectiveness.

Microorganisms and epithelial cells

Saliva, when secreted by the salivary glands, is sterile but whole saliva in the mouth may contain bacteria at levels up to 10^9/ml. For bacteria to survive in the mouth they must be able to attach to and proliferate on oral surfaces since the salivary flow rate is too high for saliva to act as a continuous culture system.[5]

Epithelial cells are continually being shed from the oral mucosa into saliva and it has been estimated that the surface cells stay attached for only about three hours before being desquamated.[5] Each epithelial cell has about 100 bacteria attached to its surface and in saliva there are about three times more bacteria bound to epithelial cells than are unattached.[5] Most of the bacteria in saliva appear to be derived from mucosal tissues rather than from the teeth. However, after a prophylaxis, and in the subsequent absence of oral hygiene, the amount of plaque on the teeth will gradually increase until an equilibrium is reached when the rate at which bacteria are being shed from plaque into saliva is equal to the rate of their proliferation on the teeth. Thus, salivary clearance plays an important role in removing bacteria and epithelial cells from the mouth and individuals with hyposalivation will have higher salivary bacterial and epithelial cell counts. In addition, salivary flow is very low during sleep (see Chapter 3), which explains why the salivary bacterial and epithelial cell counts are greatest before breakfast. Halitosis is thus usually most marked at this time of day since epithelial cells are one of the substrates from which some Gram-negative anaerobes are able to form volatile sulphur compounds with an unpleasant odour.

Some factors influencing salivary clearance

The most important variables are the residual and maximum volumes, the unstimulated and stimulated flow rates, and the extent to which the substance being cleared binds to oral surfaces.[6]

The volume of saliva left in the mouth after swallowing (residual volume)
As measured in studies on 40 normal individuals,[7] the mean residual volume is about 0.8 ml, but the large range (0.4–1.4 ml) suggests that variations in the residual volume may be responsible for some individual differences in clearance patterns. According to the Dawes computer model, the effect of varying the residual volume on clearance halftime (the time for the salivary sucrose concentration to decrease by half) after a 10% sucrose mouthrinse is very large (Fig. 5.2). In fact, the difference in concentration obtained with the lowest residual volume (0.4 ml) and the highest volume tested (1.4 ml) was more than 50-fold after only 10 minutes. Thus individuals who swallow more effectively (ie have a low residual volume) will clear substances from the mouth more quickly.

The volume of saliva in the mouth just prior to swallowing (maximum volume)
Another important physiological variable affecting salivary clearance is the maximum volume of saliva allowed to accumulate in the mouth before swallowing is initiated. The mean value in 40 individuals was 1.1 ml, but as with the residual volume, a wide range (0.5–2.1 ml) was found, those with larger residual volumes naturally having larger maximum volumes.[7] Again, a

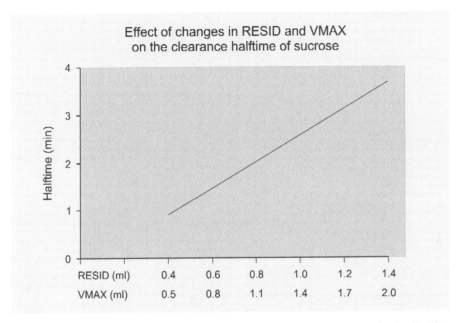

Fig. 5.2 A computer simulation of the effect of changes in the residual volume after swallowing (Resid) and the maximum volume before swallowing (Vmax) on the clearance halftime of sucrose after a 10% sucrose mouthrinse. The clearance halftime is the time for the concentration to fall by half.

large effect on the clearance halftime is seen (Fig. 5.2), and individuals who do not allow as much saliva to accumulate in the mouth before swallowing will clear substances more rapidly.

The unstimulated salivary flow rate

The unstimulated salivary flow rate is normally about 0.3–0.4 ml/min but may vary a great deal among individuals (*see* Chapter 3). Since the swallowing frequency is dependent on the rate of entry of saliva into the mouth, it is obvious that the salivary flow rate is an extremely important variable. According to the Dawes model, the lower the unstimulated salivary flow rate, the more prolonged will be the clearance halftime for sucrose (Fig. 5.3). Since individuals with severe hyposalivation may have unstimulated flow rates even lower than the minimum value of 0.05 ml/min shown in the figure, the delayed clearance of carbohydrate may help to account for their high susceptibility to dental caries.

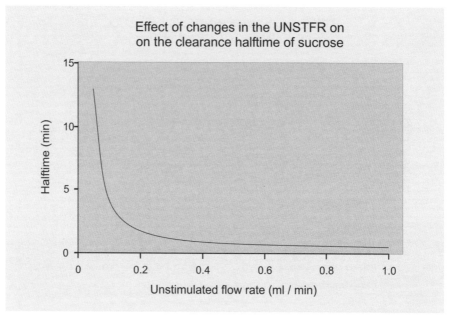

Fig. 5.3 A computer simulation of the effect of changes in the unstimulated flow rate on the clearance of sucrose after a 10% sucrose mouthrinse. The simulation assumed average values for the unstimulated flow rate (0.32 ml/min), Resid (0.8 ml), and Vmax (1.1 ml). The curve approximates a rectangular hyperbola so that clearance is greatly prolonged at low flow rates.

The stimulated salivary flow rate

Although salivary flow may remain above the unstimulated rate for only about a minute after food consumption or after a sucrose rinse, the initial rate at which the sucrose is diluted plays a critical role in determining how much sucrose diffuses into dental plaque. The longer the salivary sucrose concentration remains high, the more sucrose will diffuse into dental plaque. In individuals with a normal unstimulated flow rate, the salivary sucrose concentration will have fallen so low within the first two or three minutes after a sucrose rinse that a rinse with water at that time would have little influence on acid production in plaque (see later).

Lagerlöf has shown, in a computer model, that the stimulated flow rate can also have a great effect on the clearance pattern of fluoride.[4] As with sucrose, the faster clearance rate caused by stimulation of salivary flow reduces the amount of fluoride diffusing into dental plaque. In formulating cariostatic

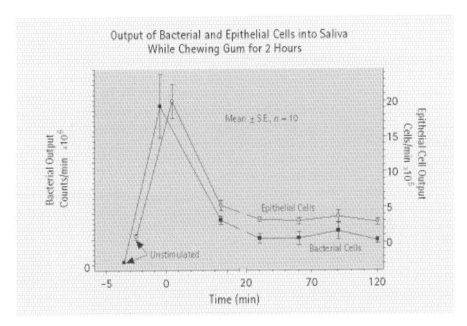

Fig. 5.4 Output of bacterial and epithelial cells into saliva while chewing gum for two hours. To avoid overlap of data, the results for bacterial cells over the –5–0 minute period (unstimulated) and the 0–1 minute period of chewing have been set back on the abscissa by one minute.

topical fluoride products, such as fluoride tablets, it thus seems advisable to use agents that do not stimulate salivation, in other words, ones that are tasteless. Tablets should be allowed to dissolve slowly in the mouth rather than be chewed.

Many investigators measure bacterial counts on saliva samples elicited by chewing on paraffin wax but with inadequate control of the flow rate or duration of chewing. However, as seen in Figure 5.4, when sequential saliva samples are collected, there is an enormous peak in the output of both bacteria and epithelial cells at the initiation of the chewing process.[8] Lack of control of the saliva collection conditions thus makes interpretation of salivary bacterial counts very difficult.

Use of products such as chewing gum causes an initial increase in salivary flow rate to about 12 times the unstimulated rate and with prolonged chewing the flow rate remains at two to three times the unstimulated rate. Surprisingly, the use of chewing gum does not greatly increase the degree of mixing of the different salivary secretions but the increased flow rate does speed up the clearance process.

Saliva as a film

For too long, oral biologists have generally thought of dental plaque as being covered by a large volume of saliva, the composition of which remains essentially constant unless the flow rate changes. In fact, for most of the time, saliva is present as a very thin film whose composition changes locally when materials diffuse into or out of dental plaque. Given an average volume of saliva in the mouth of about 1 ml, and that the surface area of the adult mouth is just over 200 cm^2, the saliva must be present as a film averaging about 0.1 mm or less in thickness between adjacent surfaces.[9]

Recent studies[10,11] have shown marked site-specificity in the thickness of the salivary film with values on individual surfaces ranging from 70 µm on the posterior dorsum of the tongue to 10 µm on the anterior hard palate. Film thicknesses of <10 µm in the latter location are associated with reports of mouth dryness. In patients who report that their mouth is very dry, the residual volume still averages 71% of normal, which suggests that dry mouth is not due to complete oral dryness but to localized areas of dryness, notably on the anterior hard palate and tongue.

When flow is unstimulated the film has been estimated to move at different rates (0.8–8 mm/min) in different regions of the mouth.[12] These extremely slow velocities have important implications for the clearance of ingested carbohydrate and topical fluoride, but particularly for clearance of acid from dental plaque. Figure 5.5 shows the postulated directions of flow of the salivary film.

Clearance of substances from local sites

Ingested carbohydrate
Dental caries is caused by the demineralizing effects of organic acids produced in dental plaque by microorganisms that ferment carbohydrates, most notably sucrose. The Stephan curve is the fall and subsequent rise in plaque pH which occurs after exposure of dental plaque to fermentable carbohydrate (*see* Fig. 6.1). In regions of the mouth where clearance is rapid, less sucrose will be available to diffuse into dental plaque, and thus less acid will be formed.

Studies have shown that sucrose ingested in several different forms is distributed very unevenly around the mouth and is cleared at very different rates in different locations.[13–17] In general, clearance is more rapid from lingual than from buccal tooth surfaces, except buccal to the upper molars where

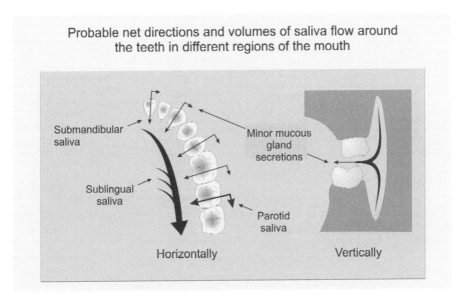

Probable net directions and volumes of saliva flow around the teeth in different regions of the mouth

Fig. 5.5 Diagrammatic representation of the anticipated directions and volumes of salivary flow in different locations in the mouth.

parotid saliva enters the mouth. Apart from that region, buccal tooth surfaces are mostly exposed to the extremely viscous secretions from the minor mucous glands. In contrast, lingual surfaces are exposed mainly to the secretions from two of the major salivary glands, namely the submandibular and sublingual.

Figure 5.6 illustrates mean results on 10 subjects for the clearance of sucrose from whole saliva and from six specific oral sites after a 10% sucrose mouthrinse.[16] Because the ordinate is a logarithmic scale, a change of one unit represents a 10-fold change in concentration. The higher the salivary film velocity in a given region, the lower is the initial concentration of sucrose and the more rapid is its clearance. Compare, for instance, clearance from the lingual of the lower incisors with that from the facial of the lower molars, where the salivary film velocities, when flow is unstimulated, have been estimated to average 8 mm/min and 1 mm/min, respectively.

Topical fluoride
The current view of fluoride's role in demineralization and remineralization of enamel stresses the value of raising slightly the fluoride level in the liquid

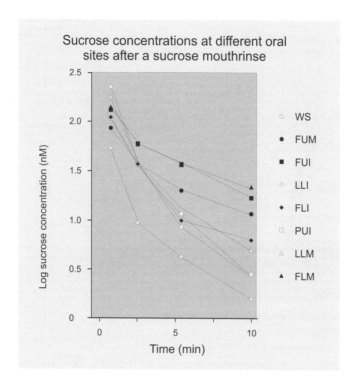

Sucrose concentrations at different oral sites after a sucrose mouthrinse

Log sucrose concentration (nM)

Time (min)

○ WS
● FUM
■ FUI
◇ LLI
◆ FLI
□ PUI
△ LLM
▲ FLM

Fig. 5.6 Sucrose concentrations in saliva at different sites and times after a 10% sucrose mouthrinse. WS = whole saliva; FUM = facial upper molars; FUI = facial upper incisors; LLI = lingual lower incisors; FLI = facial lower incisors; PUI = palatal upper incisors; LLM = lingual lower molars; FLM = facial lower molars.

surrounding the enamel crystals and for prolonged periods of time (*see* Chapter 8). To be effective, only a small increase in salivary fluoride concentration is needed above the normal value of about 1 μmol/l (0.019 ppm). This certainly occurs during, and for a certain time after, the use of dentifrices, which usually contain about 1000 ppm F, and during other preventive applications of fluoride. Those sites where the salivary film velocity is low have been shown to clear fluoride more slowly,[18] which will facilitate its anticariogenic action at the sites most susceptible to caries.

Acid from dental plaque

When plaque is exposed to sugar, the bacteria in plaque form acid, which will tend to diffuse toward the tooth surface but also out of the plaque, down its concentration gradient into saliva. A computer model of this process[19] suggested that if the salivary film is moving slowly over plaque, acid will accumulate in the film and reduce the concentration gradient between the

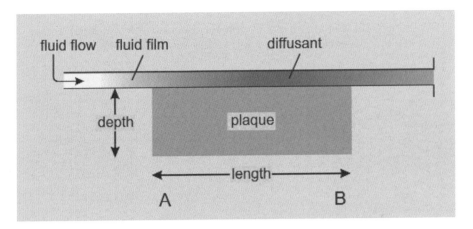

Fig. 5.7 Diagrammatic representation of the flow of a slowly moving film of saliva over dental plaque and the accumulation of a diffusant (such as organic acid) in the film at the distal edge of the plaque.

plaque and the saliva, which will retard the diffusion of acid out of the plaque (Fig. 5.7). These predictions of the computer model[20] were tested in a physical model in which 10% sucrose was passed for one minute over a 0.5 mm-deep artificial plaque of *Streptococcus oralis* (with the same acid-forming ability and buffering capacity as natural plaque), followed by unstimulated saliva at one of three different film velocities and with a film thickness of 0.1 mm. The film velocities of 0.8 and 8 mm/min are, respectively, the lowest and highest mean values estimated in the mouth when salivary flow is unstimulated, while 86 mm/min is about 10 times higher than the latter. The resulting Stephan curves (Fig. 5.8) at positions A and B (*see* Fig. 5.7) on the undersurfaces of the plaque were much deeper and more prolonged at the lowest film velocity, especially at position B. Thus oral regions with a more slowly moving salivary film (eg buccal to the upper incisors – velocity 0.8 mm/min) might be more susceptible to caries than regions with a faster moving salivary film (eg lingual to the lower incisors – velocity 8 mm/min) because acid is cleared away from plaque more slowly at a low film velocity.

The effect on the Stephan curve of a mouthrinse with water

It has often been reported that rinsing the mouth with water after eating or drinking sugary items does not significantly reduce the fall in plaque pH, suggesting perhaps that the role of saliva in the clearance of sugar and in the

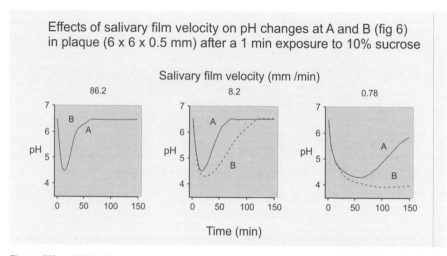

Effects of salivary film velocity on pH changes at A and B (fig 6) in plaque (6 x 6 x 0.5 mm) after a 1 min exposure to 10% sucrose

Fig. 5.8 Effect of fluid film velocity on the pH at position A (see Fig. 5.7), where the plaque is first contacted by fresh saliva, and at position B (see Fig. 5.7), where the salivary film leaves the plaque, under an artificial plaque 6 mm square and 0.5 mm deep after exposure to a 10% sucrose solution for one minute.

clearance of plaque acid, by diffusion into saliva, has been overestimated. By contrast, stimulation of salivary flow by the chewing of sugar-free chewing gum, which increases the bicarbonate concentration in saliva, is very effective in restoring plaque pH to neutrality (*see* Fig. 6.4). This could suggest that the salivary effect is due only to the buffering power of the bicarbonate in saliva, rather than to the enhanced clearance of sugar or acid.

However, the lack of effect of mouthrinsing with water on the Stephan curve may be partly because it is generally done too late: a few minutes after a sucrose challenge, the sugar concentration in saliva is usually lower than that in plaque, so rinsing with water at that time would not be expected to reduce the diffusion of sugar into plaque, unless the sugar clearance were excessively slow, as in patients with hyposalivation. As far as the removal of acid is concerned, outward diffusion of hydrogen ions alone does not adequately explain plaque neutralization. Shellis and Dibdin[21] have shown that most of the H^+ ions in dental plaque are fixed to bacterial surface proteins and other fixed buffers. That is why mobile salivary buffers such as bicarbonate and phosphate, which are present in the salivary film (but not in a water rinse), are so important – they are able to diffuse into plaque as HCO_3^- and HPO_4^{2-} ions, capture the hydrogen ions from the fixed buffers, and diffuse out into the saliva as H_2CO_3 and as $H_2PO_4^-$ ions.

The advantage of mouthrinsing after meals then is that it helps to remove food debris as well as sugars in solution and this may be particularly valuable in individuals with hyposalivation in whom sugar clearance may be greatly delayed (Fig. 5.3).

The site-specificity of dental caries and calculus deposition

In a fasted subject, the extracellular fluid phase of dental plaque (plaque fluid) is normally supersaturated with respect to several calcium phosphates, such as those in teeth and dental calculus (*see* Chapter 8). This condition favours remineralization of early caries lesions and deposition of calculus. However, when plaque is exposed to fermentable carbohydrate, the bacteria form acid, and if the pH falls below a critical value (probably about 5.1–5.5), which is inversely proportional to the calcium and phosphate concentrations in plaque fluid, the latter becomes unsaturated. At such times, the teeth will tend to dissolve (dental caries), as will the calcium phosphate crystals present in early calculus.

Dawes and Macpherson[16] have postulated that supragingival calculus forms most readily on the lingual surfaces of the lower anterior teeth and the buccal surfaces of the upper molars because these are sites with a high salivary film velocity. This will promote the development of shallow Stephan curves, because of the rapid clearance of sugar from the adjacent saliva and because of the rapid clearance of acid from dental plaque, and there will be little opportunity for calcium phosphate crystals in early calculus to dissolve during meals or snacks. They have also suggested that smooth-surface caries is much more prevalent buccally than lingually because salivary film velocity is much lower buccally than lingually. A low film velocity buccally will slow the rate of sucrose clearance from the saliva and the clearance of acid from dental plaque, which will promote the development of deep and prolonged Stephan curves and enamel dissolution, leading to dental caries.

The mouth is clearly not a uniform environment but contains many distinct micro-environments, some of which are more conducive than others to the development of oral disease.

Summary – clinical highlights

Rapid oral clearance of microorganisms, of sucrose and other carbohydrate substrates, and of acid from plaque metabolism, will be of clinical benefit to oral health. However, for protective agents like fluoride or chlorhexidine, a slow clearance is preferable. Knowledge of the factors determining clearance rates in different locations is leading to a more detailed picture of the reasons for the site-specificity of dental caries and supragingival calculus deposition and suggesting ways to maximize some benefits – for example, the avoidance of salivary stimulation during topical fluoride applications and by allowing fluoride tablets to dissolve slowly in the mouth rather than be chewed.

Acknowledgements

Thanks are due to Dr F Lagerlöf, who gave the original presentation, which formed the basis for Chapter 7 in the 1st Edition. We thank Elsevier for permission to include the data in Fig. 5.4 (Fig. 2 from *Arch Oral Biol* 2001; **46**: 625–632) and the Journal of Dental Research for permission to include Fig. 5.5 (Fig. 3 from *J Dent Res* 1987; **66** : 1614–1618).

Further reading

1   Swenander-Lanke L. Influences on salivary sugar of certain properties of foodstuffs and individual oral conditions. *Acta Odontol Scand* 1957; **15**: Supplement 23.

2   Dawes C. A mathematical model of salivary clearance of sugar from the oral cavity. *Caries Res* 1983; **17**: 321–334.

3   Aasenden R, Brudevold F, Richardson B. Clearance of fluoride from the mouth after topical treatment or the use of a fluoride mouthrinse. *Arch Oral Biol* 1968; **13**: 625–636.

4   Lagerlöf F, Oliveby A, Ekstrand J. Physiological factors influencing salivary clearance of sugar and fluoride. *J Dent Res* 1987; **66**: 430–435.

5   Dawes C. Estimates, from salivary analyses, of the turnover time of the oral mucosal epithelium in humans and the number of bacteria in an edentulous mouth. *Arch Oral Biol* 2003; **48**: 329–336.

6   Dawes C. Physiological factors affecting salivary flow rate, oral sugar clearance, and the sensation of dry mouth in man. *J Dent Res* 1987; **66**: 648–653.

7   Lagerlöf F, Dawes C. The volume of saliva in the mouth before and after swallowing. *J Dent Res* 1984; **63**: 618–621.

8   Dawes C, Tsang R W L, Suelzle T. The effects of gum chewing, four oral hygiene procedures, and two saliva collection techniques, on the output of bacteria into human whole saliva. *Arch Oral Biol* 2001; **46**: 625–632.

9   Collins L M C, Dawes C. The surface area of the adult human mouth and thickness of the salivary film covering the teeth and oral mucosa. *J Dent Res* 1987; **66**: 1300–1302.

10   DiSabato T, Kleinberg I. Measurement and comparison of the residual saliva on various mucosal and dentition surfaces in humans. *Arch Oral Biol* 1996; **41**: 655–665.

11   Wolff M S, Kleinberg I. The effect of ammonium glycopyrrolate (Robinul®)-induced xerostomia on oral mucosal wetness and flow of gingival crevicular fluid in humans. *Arch Oral Biol* 1999; **44**: 97–102.

12   Dawes C, Watanabe S, Biglow-Lecomte P, Dibdin G H. Estimation of the velocity of the salivary film at some different locations in the mouth. *J Dent Res* 1989; **68**: 1479–1482.

13   Britse A, Lagerlöf F. The diluting effect of saliva on the sucrose concentration in different parts of the human mouth after a mouth-rinse with sucrose. *Arch Oral Biol* 1987; **32**: 755–756.

14   Lindfors B, Lagerlöf F. Effect of sucrose concentration in saliva after a sucrose rinse on the hydronium ion concentration in dental plaque. *Caries Res* 1988; **22**: 7–10.

15   Weatherell J A, Duggal M S, Robinson C, Curzon M E J. Site-specific differences in human dental plaque pH after sucrose rinsing. *Arch Oral Biol* 1988; **33**: 871–873.

16 Dawes C, Macpherson L M D. The distribution of saliva and sucrose around the mouth during the use of chewing gum and the implications for the site-specificity of caries and calculus deposition. *J Dent Res* 1993; **72**: 852–857.

17 Macpherson L M D, Dawes C. Distribution of sucrose around the mouth and its clearance after a sucrose mouthrinse or consumption of three different foods. *Caries Res* 1994; **28**: 150–155.

18 Weatherell J A, Strong M, Robinson C, Ralph J P. Fluoride distribution in the mouth after fluoride rinsing. *Caries Res* 1986; **20**: 111–119.

19 Dawes C. An analysis of factors influencing diffusion from dental plaque into a moving film of saliva and the implications for caries. *J Dent Res* 1989; **68**: 1483–1488.

20 Macpherson L M D, Dawes C. Effects of salivary film velocity on pH changes in an artificial plaque containing *Streptococcus oralis*, after exposure to sucrose. *J Dent Res* 1991; **70**: 1230–1234.

21 Shellis R P, Dibdin G H. Analysis of the buffering systems in dental plaque. *J Dent Res* 1988; **67**: 438–446.

Saliva and the control of plaque pH

Michael Edgar and Susan M Higham

The Stephan curve

Acidogenic bacteria in dental plaque can rapidly metabolize certain carbohydrates to acid end products. In the mouth, the resultant change in plaque pH over time is called a Stephan curve (Fig. 6.1). Under resting conditions the pH is fairly constant although differences among individuals, and among sites in one individual, are found. Following exposure of the plaque to fermentable carbohydrate the pH decreases rapidly to reach a minimum after approximately 5–20 minutes before slowly returning to its starting value over 30–60 minutes or even longer.

Resting plaque pH

The term 'resting plaque' refers to plaque 2–2.5 hours after the last intake of dietary carbohydrate as opposed to 'starved plaque' which has not been exposed to carbohydrates for 8–12 hours. Resting plaque pH is usually between 6 and 7 whereas the starved plaque pH is normally between 7 and 8. A large range of plaque pH values seem to be compatible with oral health, but due to the multifactorial nature of dental caries, what may be healthy for one individual may be unhealthy for another.

Resting plaque contains relatively high concentrations of acetate compared with lactate. The predominant free amino acids in plaque are glutamate and proline, with ammonia also found at significant levels.[1] The presence of elevated levels of acetate is due to the accumulation of end products of amino acid breakdown as well as those of carbohydrate metabolism. These metabolic products are present at much higher concentrations than in saliva. This is partly due to the fact that they are constantly produced from the metabolism of intracellular and extracellular bacterial carbohydrate stores, and from the breakdown of salivary glycoproteins. Their diffusion out of plaque is hindered by the slow salivary film velocity (*see* Chapter 5) under 'resting' conditions when saliva is unstimulated.

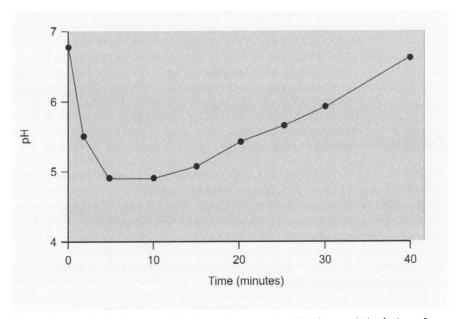

Fig. 6.1 Diagram of a Stephan curve – the plaque pH response to a 10% glucose solution (redrawn from Jenkins, The physiology and biochemistry of the mouth. London: Blackwell, 1978).

The decrease in plaque pH

Two main factors affect the rate at which the plaque pH decreases:
1. The presence of exogenous, rapidly fermentable carbohydrate, usually sugars.

2. Low buffering capacity of saliva at unstimulated flow rates.

The fall in pH has been related to the production of principally lactic acid.[2] Simultaneously, acetatic and proprionic acids are lost from the plaque. These acids were assumed to be lost to the saliva but there are indications that they may diffuse also from the plaque into the tooth.[3] In terms of the pH change in plaque, the amount of a low pK acid such as lactate relative to a higher pK acid such as acetate is very important. The high pK acids can provide a buffering system because they can absorb the hydrogen ions generated by dissociation of the low pK acids. The fall in pH could thus be enhanced by a reduction of

87

the buffering power of plaque acetate. The nature of the acids in plaque may be important because they differ in their ability to attack enamel. As the pH of plaque decreases, the concentrations of amino acids and ammonia in plaque also fall rapidly.[1] This fall may be due to the bacterial uptake and utilization of nitrogenous material for anabolic reactions, stimulated by the availability of energy from carbohydrate fermentation.

The minimum plaque pH

The minimum value of plaque pH and how long the pH stays at that minimum are determined by several factors:

1. Whether any fermentable carbohydrate remains in the mouth, and whether the carbohydrate has been cleared from the mouth, eg by swallowing, rather than being metabolized by plaque bacteria.

2. The pH may fall to values at which bacterial enzyme systems are no longer functioning properly.

3. The buffering capacity, both in plaque and saliva but particularly in stimulated saliva, may be critical.

The minimum pH corresponds with the greatest concentration of lactate produced during a Stephan curve and with a reduction in acetate, succinate, propionate, most of the amino acids, and ammonia.

The length of time that the pH remains at its minimum is important since if it reaches the so-called 'critical pH', which is the pH at which saliva and plaque fluid cease to be saturated with respect to enamel mineral, then the dissolution of enamel may ensue (*see* Chapter 8). The pH minimum usually occurs after salivation ceases to be stimulated, and although the buffering power of post-stimulated saliva remains higher than that of unstimulated saliva for some minutes, it eventually falls: this fall in salivary buffering may coincide with the minimum pH in plaque, thus allowing it to remain low. The benefit of continued stimulation of saliva throughout the Stephan curve is discussed below.

The rise in plaque pH

The steady rise in pH back to the resting value is influenced by all the factors mentioned above, including diffusion of acids out of the plaque into saliva. It

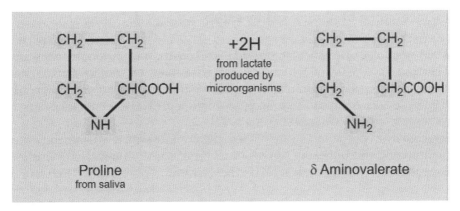

Fig. 6.2 The Stickland reaction.

is also influenced by base production in plaque. Ammonia is highly alkaline and can thus neutralize acid and cause a rise in pH. It is derived mainly from the breakdown of salivary urea (*see* Chapter 1) but also from the deamination of amino acids. Another group of basic products in plaque are amines – formed from amino acids by decarboxylation. These bases are thought to have an important neutralizing action in plaque, especially under conditions of moderate carbohydrate intake.

Glutamate is the predominant amino acid in plaque during the Stephan curve.[1] It is an extremely important amino acid since it is able to act as an amino donor in the synthesis of many amino acids from organic acid precursors – these amino acids are all less acidic than the corresponding organic acid. Delta-amino n-valeric acid (DAVA) has been shown to be present in plaque: its concentration is lowest around the plaque pH minimum after a sucrose challenge.[1] It is formed by the reduction of proline in the Stickland reaction (Fig. 6.2). Its importance as a pH regulator, in addition to its basicity due to the amino group, is because its formation utilizes reduced NAD from the breakdown of lactate. The pH rise may also be assisted by the removal of acids. Bacteria of the genus *Veillonella* metabolize lactate to less acidic products. Acids may also diffuse into enamel and thus no longer influence plaque pH.[3]

Any residual dietary carbohydrate, as well as bacterially stored carbohydrate, may be broken down during the pH rise phase, thus slowing the process. Although the pH approaches the resting value after 30–60 minutes, the organic acid profile does not return to the resting state for several hours.

Maintenance of plaque pH by saliva

Many years ago, researchers compared the Stephan curves produced following a sucrose rinse, with and without salivary restriction. The results showed that by excluding saliva, by cannulating the ducts of the major glands and diverting their secretions out of the mouth, the minimum pH was lower and the return to the resting value delayed (Fig. 6.3).

Regulation of the intra-oral pH by saliva can be largely attributed to the neutralizing and buffering actions of its bicarbonate content, with smaller contributions from phosphate, and other factors.

Bicarbonate

This is the most important buffering system in stimulated saliva. Metabolically derived bicarbonate increases in concentration with increased salivary gland activity, so that bicarbonate provides an increasingly effective buffer system against plaque acid, especially at high flow rates when concentrations may reach up to 60 mmol/l. The rise in bicarbonate concentration also leads to a rise in salivary pH, which directly neutralizes the plaque acidity.

Phosphate

In unstimulated saliva, concentrations of phosphate may peak at around 10 mmol/l. These concentrations fall, however, at high rates of flow, and the phosphate system is of minor importance as a buffer. The protective role of salivary phosphate is due more to its contribution to the saturation of saliva with respect to enamel mineral (*see* Chapter 8).

Other factors

As seen above, saliva contains urea at concentrations similar to those in blood. Many plaque bacteria possess urease activity, converting urea to ammonia, thus raising plaque pH. Saliva also contains peptides, known as 'pH rise factors', which have been suggested to maintain plaque pH. The best-established of these is a basic peptide containing arginine which has been named 'sialin'.[4] Some bacteria can decarboxylate the amino acids from such peptides to form basic amines. Base production in the form of ammonia and amines is responsible for the fact that the pH of starved plaque is often higher than that of the saliva bathing it.

Urea has been added to chewing gum to increase salivary concentrations and raise the pH of plaque. Recently, salivary concentrations of urea after chewing

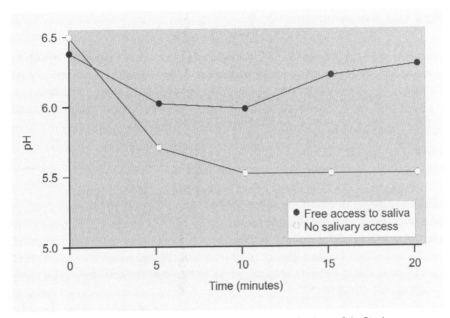

Fig. 6.3 The effect of restricting the access of saliva to plaque upon the shape of the Stephan curve (redrawn from Jenkins, The physiology and biochemistry of the mouth. London: Blackwell, 1978).

urea-containing gum were measured and their effect on an artificial 'Stephan Curve' evaluated. The beneficial effect of urea was shown to occur only after a sucrose challenge – if the gum was chewed before the challenge there was no reduction in plaque pH fall.[5]

Buffering capacity of plaque

Plaque has intrinsic 'fixed' buffering capacity due mainly to bacterial proteins and other macromolecules in plaque. These fixed buffers are in equilibrium with 'mobile' buffers – phosphates and bicarbonate – which exchange with those in saliva (*see* Chapter 3). Calcium phosphate crystals are thought to be present even in young plaque and can dissolve under acid conditions to increase greatly the buffering capacity. This can also raise the concentrations of calcium and phosphate ions, and thus help to oppose the demineralization of the tooth. A negative correlation exists between calcium phosphates in plaque, and caries activity.[6]

91

Age and site of plaque

The age and site of plaque in the mouth are important considerations in plaque pH studies since they influence the chemical and microbial composition and thickness of plaque, and the access of saliva to the plaque. The age of plaque is usually defined as the time elapsed since plaque was last removed, for example, by professional or by very thorough home tooth cleaning. This definition is limited, however, because plaque is constantly being disturbed and removed by the action of tongue, lips and cheeks, and by foods. The thickness of plaque is therefore a more rational parameter, although difficult to measure. Thickness affects microbial composition, and the velocity of diffusion of substances through plaque. Thicker plaques are more anaerobic, and so in their inner layers will favour the growth of more strictly anaerobic bacterial species. The rate of penetration of nutrients into, and metabolic products out of plaque will vary inversely with the square of the thickness of plaque, and also on the molecular size and charge of the diffusing substance. Calcium and phosphate levels in plaque increase with time; 10-day-old plaque has about 25% of the mineral content of calculus. Most plaque pH studies use plaque in subjects who have refrained from oral hygiene procedures for 24 or 48 hours.

It is sometimes suggested that toothbrushing may be more effective before meals, as the residual plaque is too thin to lead to a large drop in pH, and with fluoride dentifrice the metabolism of plaque bacteria will be inhibited. However, the salivary stimulation during eating is known to accelerate the clearance of fluoride from the mouth, and this disadvantage may outweigh the advantages of brushing before meals.

Diet history

The dietary history of plaque is one of the most important factors affecting the Stephan curve. Even a modest restriction of sugar intake for 1–2 days will considerably influence the shape of the curve. For example, when plaque pH in humans is compared before and after a sequence of sucrose rinses over three weeks, there is a decrease in both resting and minimum pH. Many oral bacteria produce extracellular polysaccharides in the presence of excess sucrose. These include glucans, which are thought to increase plaque adhesion and thickness, as well as fructans, which are subsequently broken down to acid. Some bacteria form intracellular polysaccharide stores, the breakdown of which is an ongoing contribution to acid production in resting plaque.

Plaque pH and salivary clearance

Salivary clearance refers to the dilution and removal of substances from the mouth (*see* Chapter 5). The flow rate of saliva has the greatest influence on the rate of clearance – the faster the flow, the faster the clearance rate. Patients with rapid clearance rates have a shallow Stephan curve, whereas those whose clearance is slow have deeper curves as lower pH values are reached.[7]

Studies have shown that the labial and upper anterior region is a site of slow clearance, the lingual and lower anterior region a site of rapid clearance, and the buccal area a site of intermediate clearance. The plaque pH in these regions relates well to the rate of clearance. The approximal surfaces of the upper anteriors have the lowest plaque pH, since clearance is slower from these sites. This also relates to the caries prevalence in anterior teeth, being higher in upper than lower approximal surfaces.

The residual volume of saliva after swallowing has been found to be important in determining the clearance rate: the smaller the residual volume, the faster the clearance (*see* Chapter 5). A significant positive correlation between the residual volume of saliva and the caries experience of an individual has been found.[8]

Plaque pH in renal dialysis patients

Children on renal dialysis have high concentrations of ammonia and urea in saliva compared with normal children. In one study it was found that although the children on dialysis ate many sweets, they had a lower caries experience than control children. It is likely that this is due to a direct effect of salivary urea and ammonia on plaque pH, as plaque from these children was capable of forming acid when incubated with sugars after removal from the oral cavity. A recent study has shown significantly higher plaque pH in children with chronic renal failure compared with controls, in parallel with the raised salivary urea concentration (mean, 11.6 mmol/l compared with 3.6 mmol/l). In addition, the number of mutans streptococci isolated from the renal patients was significantly lower.[9]

Plaque pH and fluoride levels

Salivary fluoride levels, even in a fluoridated area and with the use of fluoride dentifrice, are quite low, about 0.5–2.0 μmol/l (0.01–0.04 mg/l) although immediately after brushing the concentration from dentifrice is much higher (100–200 mg/l) and a small increase (around 0.05 mg/l) is detectable in the saliva of fluoride dentifrice users 18 hours after brushing. These minor changes in salivary fluoride can lead to increased levels of fluoride in plaque. Plaque fluoride concentrations are high for up to 8 hours after a fluoride rinse – ie they are retained directly from the rinse and not recycled via saliva. Fluoride levels in plaque are usually 50–100 times higher than those in whole saliva.

Systemic fluorides have only a small effect on plaque acid production, but their effect may be great enough to tip the scales between demineralization and remineralization of the tooth enamel. Part of the fluoride in plaque is in bound form, but is released into the plaque fluid when the pH falls. This can be potentially beneficial in favouring remineralization and modifying subsequent bacterial metabolism.

Topically administered fluorides have antibacterial actions but this is a direct effect and not mediated by saliva. However, fluoride from dentifrices, gels and other vehicles may bind to the soft tissues or precipitate on the tooth surface as calcium fluoride, which then slowly dissolves into the saliva leading to the raised concentrations noted above.

Fluoride-containing chewing gum has been investigated as an anticaries product for daily use; doses range from 0.1–0.5 mg F as sodium fluoride. Salivary fluoride concentrations are elevated, especially on the chewing side, and may promote increased remineralization of enamel and dentine.[10]

Salivary stimulation and plaque pH

The knowledge that saliva is beneficial in terms of plaque pH and buffering following consumption of a cariogenic food has provoked much interest in agents which stimulate an increase in salivary flow. Chewing gum has been tested in plaque pH studies, with sugar-free gum producing a rise in plaque pH reflecting the raised pH of stimulated saliva. With a sugar-containing gum, a fall in plaque pH occurred which lasted for 20 minutes (Fig. 6.4). The use of chewing gum would seem to have a beneficial effect on plaque pH by stimulating salivary flow, but this effect may be reduced by the presence of fermentable carbohydrates. If

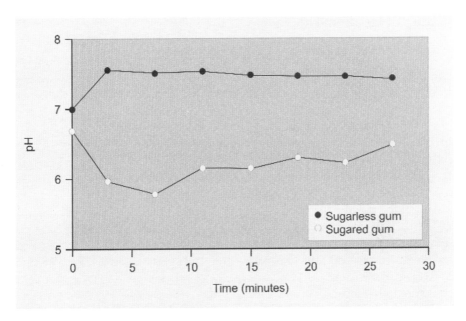

Fig. 6.4 Plaque pH responses to chewing sugarless or sugared chewing gum (redrawn from Rugg-Gunn et al., Br Dent J 1978; 145: 95-100).

sugar-containing gum is chewed after meals or snacks which contain fermentable carbohydrate, it can exert a pH raising effect, but this is smaller than with sugar-free gum (Fig. 6.5). Chewing sugar-free gum to stimulate salivation not only raises plaque pH after carbohydrate intakes, but may increase stimulated saliva flow, pH and buffering power, and both resting and post-sucrose plaque pH when chewed vigorously every hour for two weeks, suggesting an increase in gland function.[11]

Chewing an unflavoured material such as paraffin wax following consumption of a fermentable carbohydrate leads to a marked rise in plaque pH similar to that with sugar-free chewing gum accompanied by consistent decreases in the concentrations of lactate and acetate and increases in many amino acids (Fig. 6.6). The rise in pH during chewing was closely associated with the increase in saliva flow and bicarbonate buffering but may also involve other factors including an increased supply of nitrogenous material for base production. The chewing of cheese, a food rich in nitrogenous substrates, also elicits a rise in plaque pH similar to that with paraffin wax (Fig. 6.6), despite the pH of the cheese bolus being acidic. Not only is the pH of plaque raised to

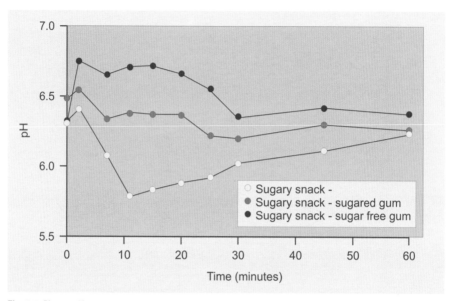

Fig. 6.5 Plaque pH responses to a sugary snack alone, and followed by sugared or sugar-free gum (redrawn from Manning and Edgar, Br Dent J 1993; 174: 241–244).

less damaging levels in terms of enamel demineralization, but also the plaque fluid concentrations of strong acids fall and neutral and basic products rise. It is likely that part of the effect of cheese can be explained by the breakdown of cheese proteins, notably casein, but other factors may be involved including the fact that cheese is a strong sialogogue. Cheese also raises the plaque concentrations of calcium and phosphate.

Similar plaque pH effects have been found with chewing gum containing urea, and urea rinses. Some studies of plaque pH use the technique of chewing paraffin wax or using a urea rinse to bring the plaque pH back up to resting levels after a carbohydrate challenge. Figure 6.7 shows the effect of a range of sucrose concentrations (0.05–10%) on plaque pH. At 0.05%, there was a small decrease in plaque pH which returned to resting values quite quickly, even without the aid of a paraffin chew. However, at higher sucrose concentrations, the pH only returned to normal after a urea rinse, indicating that continuing sugar metabolism was taking place in the plaque.

These results show that simple measurement of pH does not necessarily indicate the metabolic processes going on in the plaque; just because the plaque

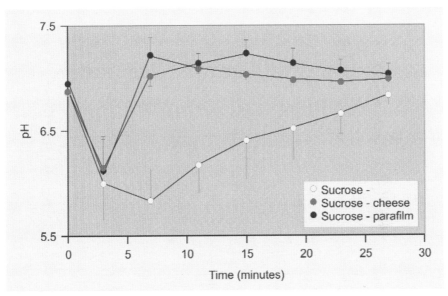

Fig. 6.6 Plaque pH responses to a sucrose mouthrinse alone, and followed by paraffin or cheese (redrawn from Higham and Edgar, Caries Res 1989; 23: 42–48).

pH is 7 does not mean that there is no carbohydrate breakdown occurring in the plaque. This implies that the pH should be monitored over an extended period. Determination of the concentrations of the acid end products of metabolism gives a more direct indication of plaque activity in the mouth.

Salivary pH can show a fall after a carbohydrate challenge, as well as plaque pH. Although stimulated saliva is normally more alkaline than unstimulated, after some challenges the formation of acid in the mouth, not only by plaque organisms but also by bacteria on soft tissues, eg the tongue, can be so rapid that the buffering capacity of the saliva is overcome and the salivary pH can fall to as low as 5.0. This will reduce the protective buffering of plaque by saliva.

Plaque pH in caries-free and caries-susceptible subjects.

Caries-free subjects, or those with minimal caries, tend to have a slightly higher resting plaque pH, a higher minimum pH following consumption of fermentable carbohydrate, and a faster return to resting levels, when compared with caries-susceptible subjects. When saliva is excluded, however, the

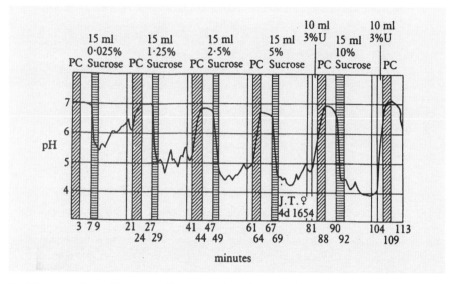

Fig. 6.7 Plaque pH recordings from an interdental electrode in a partial denture after rinsing with increasing concentrations of sucrose solution. PC = paraffin chewing; U = urea 3% rinse. (Reproduced from Imfeld, Schweitz Monats Zahn 1977; 87: 448).

differences between caries-free and caries-susceptible subjects are less marked and the minimum pH values reached are lower (Fig. 6.8). These findings indicate the importance of saliva as a factor determining caries susceptibility by modifying the plaque pH response.

Plaque from caries-free subjects produces more base than plaque from caries-susceptible subjects: these bases include polyamines and ammonia. The levels of free arginine and free lysine in stimulated parotid saliva from caries-free adults have been found to be significantly higher than those from subjects with caries experience.[12]

Clinical implications of salivary stimulation

There is a wealth of evidence supporting the benefits of stimulating saliva following eating to enhance its protective role in dental health. In recent years the use of chewing gum as a salivary stimulant has received much attention since it has been shown to produce a continued flow of saliva during prolonged mastication.

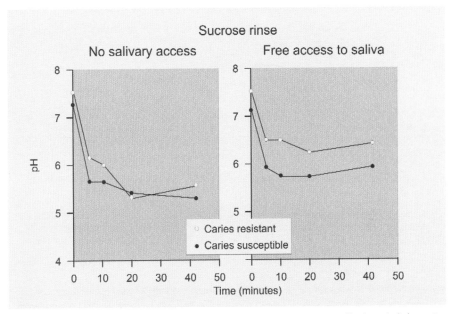

Fig. 6.8 Stephan curves from caries–free and caries–susceptible subjects when saliva is excluded or not excluded. (Redrawn from Abelson and Mandel, J Dent Res 1981; 60: 1634–1638).

The use of sugar-free chewing gum has been found to be particularly valuable.[13] Clinical evidence suggests that these products are non-cariogenic, and that when they are chewed after meals they may reduce the cariogenic effects of other foods. Sugar-free gum can be chewed for a prolonged period without increasing the calorific content of the diet. Using an intra-oral caries model system, artificial enamel lesions were remineralized more effectively when subjects chewed sugar-free gum after meals and snacks than in controls who did not chew gum. Clinical trials of the use of sorbitol-sweetened gum after meals and snacks have revealed reductions in caries incidence of between 10 and 40%.

In most clinical studies, gum sweetened with xylitol has produced greater reductions in caries incidence than sorbitol-sweetened gum, although this is not a universal finding. While part of the beneficial effect of xylitol gum can be attributed to salivary stimulation, its superiority over sorbitol gum found in most studies has been attributed to the antibacterial effects of xylitol, especially on mutans streptococci. After two weeks of gum chewing, the plaque

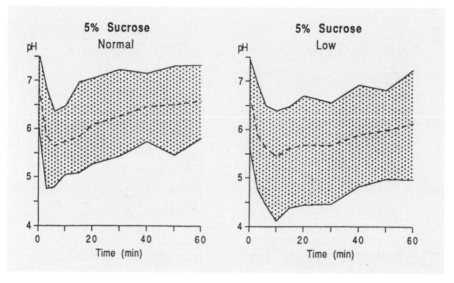

Fig. 6.9 Individual variations in plaque pH in subjects with normal and low salivary secretion rates after sucrose mouthrinsing. Shaded areas represent inter-subject variation. (Reproduced from Lingstrom and Birkhed, Acta Odont Scand 1993; 51: 379-388).

pH response to sucrose has been shown to be smaller with xylitol gum than with sorbitol gum. Maternal use of xylitol gum was associated with reduced caries incidence in their offspring during their first five years of life; this effect cannot be attributed to salivary stimulation and was associated with reduced mutans streptococcal infection of the neonates by their mothers.[14]

Plaque pH and salivary gland hypofunction

Patients suffering from xerostomia due to salivary gland hypofunction are often recommended to chew sugar-free gum, partly to relieve their symptoms but also to stimulate the function of the residual active secretory tissue (see Chapter 4). Studies have shown that subjects with salivary hypofunction could still benefit from chewing sorbitol-sweetened gum after a 10% sucrose challenge through the protective effects of the saliva produced by stimulation of their residual gland function.[15]

The protective effects of saliva can be clearly observed when comparisons are made between subjects with normal and low salivary secretion rates,

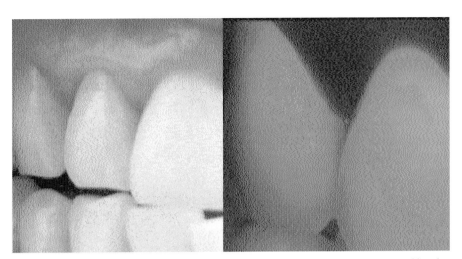

Fig. 6.10 Images of a tooth viewed in white light and by QLF. An initial lesion is present, detectable only by loss of fluorescence. (Unpublished data, Higham, Edgar and Pretty).

following consumption of fermentable carbohydrates. The low salivary flow rate accentuates the pH decrease in dental plaque (Fig. 6.9).

The early diagnosis of caries in patients with salivary gland hypofunction is likely to be enhanced by the use of quantitative light-induced fluorescence. This is a novel diagnostic device, which is able to detect very early demineralization at a stage before it can be visualized clinically (Fig. 6.10). This will encourage remineralizing therapies that increase plaque pH and salivary flow to be prescribed.

Summary – clinical highlights

- Plaque pH is a major factor controlling the equilibrium between demineralization and remineralization of the teeth, the balance of which determines the progression or repair of initial caries.

- Plaque pH reflects the balance between the production of acids (mainly from dietary carbohydrates) and bases (mainly from salivary urea and amino acids).

- Caries susceptibility and plaque pH at different sites around the mouth are related – the higher the pH, the lower the susceptibility.

- Caries-free individuals have a higher pH in plaque; this appears to be a result of more active base production from salivary substrates.

- Continued stimulation of saliva following a meal or snack, eg by chewing sugar-free gum, raises plaque pH, increases enamel remineralization, and reduces caries incidence.

- Patients with salivary gland hypofunction, provided they retain some secretory function, may benefit from saliva stimulation.

- Understanding by patients of the significance of the Stephan curve, and of ways by which it can be controlled, helps them to know how best to look after their teeth.

References

1   Higham S M, Edgar W M. Human dental plaque pH, and the organic acid and free amino acid profiles in plaque fluid, after sucrose rinsing. Arch Oral Biol 1989; **34**: 329–334.

2   Geddes D A M. The production of L(+) and D(-) lactic acid and volatile acids by human dental plaque and the effect of plaque buffering and acidic strength on pH. Arch Oral Biol 1972; **17**: 537–545.

3   Geddes D A M, Weetman D A, Featherstone J D B. Preferential loss of acetic acid from plaque fermentation in the presence of enamel. Caries Res 1984; **18**: 430–433.

4   Kleinberg I, Craw D, Komiyama K. Effect of salivary supernatant on the glycolytic activity of the bacteria in salivary sediment. Arch Oral Biol 1973; **18**: 787–798.

5   Dawes C, Dibdin G H. Salivary concentrations of urea released from a chewing gum containing urea and how these affect the urea content of gel-stabilised plaques and their pH after exposure to sucrose. Caries Res 2001; **35**: 344–353.

6   Ashley F P. Calcium and phosphorus concentrations of dental plaque related to dental caries in 11-14-year-old male subjects. Caries Res 1975; **9**: 351–362.

7   Lindfors B, Lagerlöf F. Effect of sucrose concentration in saliva after a sucrose rinse on the hydronium ion concentration in dental plaque. Caries Res 1988; **22**: 7–10.

8   Lagerlöf F, Dawes C. The volume of saliva in the mouth before and after swallowing. J Dent Res 1984; **63**: 618–621.

9   Al-Nowaiser A, Roberts G J, Trompeter R S, Wilson M, Lucas V S. Oral health in children with chronic renal failure. Pediatr Nephrol 2003; **18**: 39–45.

10 Sjögren K, Ruben J, Lingstrom P, Lundberg A B, Birkhed D. Fluoride and urea chewing gums in an intra-oral experimental caries model. Caries Res 2002; **36**: 64–69.

11 Dodds M W, Hsieh S C, Johnson D A. The effect of increased mastication by daily gum-chewing on salivary gland output and dental plaque acidogenicity. J Dent Res 1991; **70**: 1474–1478.

12 van Wuyckhuyse B C, Perinpanayagam H E R, Bevacqua D, Raubertas R F, Billings R J, Bowen W H, Tabak L A. Association of free arginine and lysine concentrations in human parotid saliva with caries experience. J Dent Res 1995; **74**: 686–690.

13 Edgar W M. Sugar substitutes, chewing gum and dental caries – a review. Brit Dent J 1998; **184**: 29–32.

14 Isokangas P, Söderling E, Pienihakkinen K and Alanen P. Occurrence of dental decay in children after maternal consumption of xylitol chewing gum, a follow-up from 0 to 5 years of age. J Dent Res 2000; **79**: 1885–1889.

15 Markovic N, Abelson D C, Mandel I D. Sorbitol gum in xerostomics: the effects on dental plaque pH and salivary flow rates. Gerodontol 1988; **7**: 71–75.

Further reading

Mandel I D. The role of saliva in maintaining oral homeostasis. J Am Dent Ass 1989; **119**: 398–304.

Sreebny L M. Saliva in health and disease: an appraisal and update. Int Dent J 2000; **50**: 146–161.

Tanzer J M. Xylitol chewing gum and dental caries. Int Dent J 1995; **45**: 65–76.

Edgar W M. Saliva: its secretion, composition and functions. Brit Dent J 1992; **172**: 305–312.

Amaechi B T, Higham S M Quantitative light-induced fluorescence: A potential tool for general dental assessment. J Biomed Optics 2002; **7**: 7–13.

Protective functions of saliva

Jorma Tenovuo

7

Human saliva not only lubricates oral tissues, making oral functions such as swallowing and speaking possible, but it also protects teeth and mucosal surfaces in many ways. The main protective factor is the constant flow of saliva from the mouth into the gut, and this 'flushing effect' transfers, for example, food debris as well as many endogenous and exogenous agents into the gut. These comprise both oral and exogenous, often noxious, microorganisms. Some of the exogenous bacteria and viruses as well as food-borne mutagens are detoxified or killed by innate components of human saliva. Also, some members of the commensal oral microflora and many of its harmful metabolic products are inhibited or neutralized by salivary components. Thus a proper amount of saliva, with its antimicrobial agents, is a requirement for a healthy balance between host defence and microbial attack in the human mouth.

Microorganisms in whole saliva

The human mouth is almost perfect for bacterial growth because bacteria appreciate its temperature, its humidity, the large surface areas for attachment, and various nutrients (growth-stimulating effects) presented through the saliva. This perfect environment is made possible by the constant presence of saliva, which dissolves the nutrients and also provides some substances, for example amino acids and endogenous carbohydrates, for bacterial growth.

Saliva is sterile when it enters the mouth but will continuously be contaminated by oral microorganisms until it leaves the mouth. Commensal bacteria and epithelial cells are shed from various oral surfaces where endogenous bacteria are attached and where they multiply to be detached into whole saliva, for example during chewing. The major sites of origin are tooth surfaces (dental plaque, oral biofilms), tongue surface and tonsils. However, microorganisms exist over the entire intra-oral surface area and the number of commensal species found in whole saliva ranges normally between 250–350, even among healthy individuals. Gingival, periodontal, tonsillar or mucosal inflammations may increase both the number of species and the total number of salivary microorganisms remarkably. It must be emphasized that microorganisms do not multiply in saliva itself but only on surfaces. Therefore, the salivary microflora is always just a reflection of the attached microflora in the mouth.

Considering the multitude of microbial species, the large surface areas and other growth-supporting properties in this saliva-humidated environment, it is not surprising that the number of microorganisms in whole saliva is high. It has been estimated that each milliliter of whole saliva (oral fluid) contains 10^8–10^9 microorganisms and the amount of bacteria swallowed per day is in the range of 1–3 grams! Based on these facts, it is very understandable that clearance of bacteria from the mouth into the gut is essential to prevent microbial overgrowth in the mouth – which often exists in cases of hyposalivation. In a healthy situation a dynamic equilibrium exists between oral microorganisms and us. It has been estimated that oral bacteria multiply once in approximately 3–4 hours, which emphasizes the need of salivary clearance of microbial cells into the gut (*see* Chapter 5).

Transmission of microorganisms by saliva contacts

The first microorganisms colonize infants' oral cavities immediately after delivery and the quality of flora during the first days of life is rather similar to that of the mother's vaginal flora. However, increasing exposure to external sources widens the number of species and increases the total quantity of oral microorganisms, of course, depending on the available species. The most important source of transmission into the baby's mouth is his/her mother. There are a number of ways by which mothers (and also other family members) can supply new microorganisms into the infant's developing oral flora. These include, for example 'cleaning' the pacifier (dummy) in the mother's own mouth before giving it to the baby (Fig. 7.1), tasting the food in her own mouth before feeding the baby, and kissing the baby on the lips. It would be perfectly all right to do these things if the mother's own (oral) health is qualitatively good and she does not carry abundant cariogenic microorganisms in her own saliva.

A typical example of this salivary transmission of cariogenic species is the group of mutans streptococci. Mothers with high salivary counts of mutans streptococci often infect their children's dentitions via salivary contacts by the age of 1–2 years and reliable scientific evidence shows that the earlier and the

Fig. 7.1 A pacifier (dummy) that has been contaminated by saliva for 10 seconds by a mother whose salivary counts of mutans streptococci are high ($>10^6$ CFU/ml). The dummy has been incubated in a selective growth medium for 3 days to show the adsorbed colonies of mutans streptococci.

more abundant the transmission of mutans streptococci to the baby's dentition, the higher is the caries incidence in later childhood (Fig. 7.2). This information is clinically highly relevant, since chair-side test methods can be used to screen mothers (or other family members/caretakers) with high salivary counts of mutans streptococci. High numbers can be reduced temporarily with, eg chlorhexidine or xylitol to prevent, or at least delay and diminish, the salivary transmission of these harmful bacteria from mothers to their babies.

Strong evidence also exists that periodontal pathogens, mainly anaerobic bacteria, are transferred via salivary contacts from person-to-person, often already by preschool age. More familiar infections from saliva are, for example, viruses – such as herpes simplex type 1, Epstein-Barr virus ('kissing disease') and influenza viruses.

Growth of bacteria in saliva

Saliva not only inhibits but also selectively supports the growth of certain bacterial species. This has been proven by studies of humans (and animals) who have received their nutrition by stomach tube (gavage) and they still harbour large numbers of microorganisms in their mouth. This is mainly due to the presence of saliva-borne glycoproteins, which provide carbohydrates,

Fig. 7.2 Schematic picture of a cell of Streptococcus mutans penetrating into enamel. Lactic acid (yellow 'sprays') dissolve enamel crystals and prisms after bacterial exposure to sucrose (red disaccharides).

proteins and amino acids for bacteria. However, the microbial flora in these cases is usually low in lactobacilli, mutans streptococci and yeasts but their numbers increase as soon as oral intake of fermentable sugars is frequent.

In the salivary ecosystem the microorganisms first metabolize glycoprotein-derived carbohydrates and later the proteins. Individual species grow in different types of saliva but in most cases submandibular/sublingual secretions rich in mucins are the best growth medium. To be able to grow in saliva, bacteria need to produce glycosidases and/or proteases to get nutrients to survive without external supply. Mucins are mucoglycoproteins containing protein cores with a number of attached oligosaccharide side chains. There are two mucins in saliva,[1] high molecular weight mucin glycoprotein 1 (MUC5B, previously designated MG1) and lower molecular weight mucin glycoprotein 2 (MUC7, formerly MG2). They are products of different cell populations within the submandibular-sublingual glands. Among salivary streptococci there is large variation in their ability to grow in the presence of mucins (Fig. 7.3) and this difference is related to their capacity to hydrolyse oligosaccharide side chains by glycosidases. These enzymes are seldom found in mutans streptococci. Because mucins form an integral part of biofilms on tooth surfaces, the relative proportion of various streptococci reflects the amount of mucins in salivary

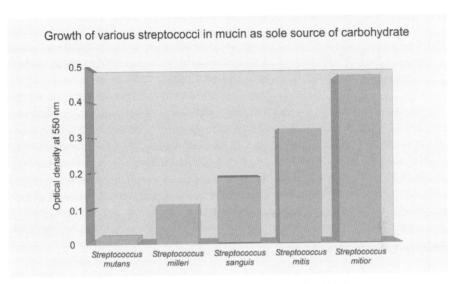

Fig. 7.3 Growth of various oral streptococci in mucin as a sole source of carbohydrate.

pellicles, ie early colonizers – such as *S. oralis* (formerly *S. mitior*), *S. mitis* and *S. sanguinis* – are dominant in early dental plaque rich in mucins. Saliva alone, without an external source of fermentable sugars, selects for a non-cariogenic microflora with low levels of mutans streptococci.

S. mutans and *S. sanguinis* both possess proteolytic activity which enables them to use the nitrogen sources in saliva (*see* Chapter 6). Free amino acids in saliva may serve as substrates for ammonia production by salivary microorganisms; ammonia is the major base in dental plaque. *S. sanguinis* can also digest arginine peptides to release arginine, which is a good source of ammonia production in the vicinity of tooth surfaces. Thus, salivary energy sources for different bacteria produce different components, which partly determine the microbial composition of oral biofilms.

Salivary components in oral biofilms

In the mouth, salivary glycoproteins are found either as a mucosal film, or on the tooth surfaces as the acquired pellicle (cell-free proteinaceous layer). Most salivary glycoproteins identified in saliva are also found in pellicle. These include mucins, amylase, lysozyme, peroxidases, salivary immunoglobulins, bacterial glycosyltransferases and proline-rich proteins (PRPs). Pellicle varies from site to site and among individuals due to the unique nature of each person's oral ecosystem and, for example, due to genetic polymorphism observed, particularly among PRPs and amylase.

Pellicle serves as a layer to which bacteria may attach and the nature of the salivary constituents in pellicle also modifies the composition of the bacterial layer, dental plaque. Dental plaque is an example of a bacterial biofilm, which is in a constant dynamic process. Attachment, growth, removal and reattachment of bacteria may occur at the same time. Because of its high content of salivary glycoproteins and its rapid rate of formation on cleaned tooth surfaces, pellicle can also be considered as a renewable lubricant, which helps to protect the teeth from attrition and abrasion.

Biological activities of salivary proteins

The salivary protein concentration is rather low, only approximately 2 mg/ml, but yet many proteins have important antimicrobial, lubricative and digestive functions. They are also involved in modulating microbial colonization of teeth and soft tissues, in providing a barrier against entry of exogenous toxins, even carcinogens, through the oral mucosa, and in modulating salivary calcium phosphate chemistry. The latter function is important for maintaining salivary supersaturation, ie maintaining the integrity of the tooth surfaces, and also for preventing adventitious calcifications in the salivary glands and in the mouth (*see* Chapter 8).

As stated previously, salivary proteins also participate in the formation of the acquired pellicle, which is not only protective but also influences the initial microbial colonization on the teeth. Base production from basic amino acids and peptides in saliva may help to neutralize plaque acids. Collectively, salivary proteins display a wide variety of functional activities (Table 7.1), which help to maintain the integrity of the mouth and also provide protection against oral and non-oral microbial infections.[2]

Protective components and systems in saliva

The main protective factor against noxious agents, endogenous and exogenous, is the salivary flow rate. Constant flow of saliva flushes untoward components from the mouth into the gut, ie clears away excess components and cells, which

Table 7.1 Salivary protein functions in the oral cavity (modified from Bowen, 1996; 2nd edition of this book)

Oral function/activity	Associated problem	Protein function
Acts as an airway	Air-borne microorganisms	Antimicrobial systems
	Dehydration	Water-retaining glycoproteins
Entry for food	Food-borne microorganisms	Antimicrobial systems
	Food toxins	Antimicrobial systems
	Soft and hard tissue abrasion	Lubrication, mucins
Speech and swallowing	Need for lubrication	Lubrication systems, mucins
Taste and digestion	–	Gustin, α-amylase, lipases
Control of endogenous and exogenous microorganisms	Colonization and infection	Innate antimicrobial systems
	Controlling pathogens and commensals	Salivary immunoglobulins
Protection of soft tissues	Toxins, carcinogens, degradative proteases	Mucin-rich protective barrier Cystatins
Protection of hard tissues	Acid damage	Inorganic compounds, fluoride, Statherin, PRPs, pellicle
Plaque acid production	Plaque pH control	Basic amino acids, urea and peptides. Buffer effect

are not able to attach to oral surfaces (*see* Chapter 5). This clearance is enhanced by salivary agglutinins,[3] which are glycoproteins with a capacity to clump bacteria into large aggregates, which are more easily flushed away by saliva and swallowed. Therefore, the term aggregation is often used synonymously with agglutination. The most potent agglutinin is a high molecular weight glycoprotein,[3] which has been found in human saliva secreted from all major salivary glands: as little as 0.1 µg of it can agglutinate 10^8–10^9 bacteria. Other known salivary agglutinins are mucins (particularly MUC5B), fibronectin and β2-microglobulin.

Major antimicrobial proteins in human saliva are listed in Table 7.2. These are usually divided into non-immune (innate) and immune (acquired) factors, the latter representing antigen-stimulated immunoglobulins. Four major types of interactions exist between salivary antimicrobial agents and oral microorganisms. These include agglutination, inhibition of adherence, bacteriostatic or bacteriocidal activity, and interference with nutrition. Although much is known of the functions of the antimicrobial proteins *in vitro*, rather limited information of their possible clinical relevance exists.[4] It seems, however, that they are important for the control of microbial overgrowth in the mouth but how selective they are against pathogens is not yet fully understood.

Lysozyme

Lysozyme is secreted into whole saliva from major and minor salivary glands, gingival crevicular fluid and salivary leukocytes. Lysozyme is present in saliva of newborn babies at levels equal to those of adults and can thus exert antimicrobial functions before tooth emergence. The classical concept of lysozyme action is based on its muramidase activity, ie the ability to hydrolyse the $\beta(1-4)$ bond between *N*-acetylmuramic acid and *N*-acetylglucosamine in the peptidoglycan layer of the bacterial cell wall. Gram-negative bacteria are more resistant to lysozyme because of their protective outer lipopolysaccharide layer.[5] Gram-positive bacteria, such as mutans streptococci, may be protected by cell-produced extracellular polysaccharides. In addition to the muramidase activity, lysozyme is a strongly cationic protein, which can activate bacterial autolysins – 'suicide packages', which can destroy the bacterial cell walls. Salivary lysozyme concentration is not related to caries incidence or prevalence.

Lactoferrin

Lactoferrin is a non-enzymatic glycoprotein which is secreted by major and minor salivary glands. Oral leukocytes also release lactoferrin into whole saliva. The biological activity of lactoferrin is attributed to its high affinity for iron (Fe^{3+}) and the consequent deprivation of this essential metal from pathogenic microorganisms. This leads to a bacteriostatic effect which is lost if the lactoferrin molecule is saturated with iron. In its iron-free state, lactoferrin (called apo-lactoferrin) also has a bactericidal, irreversible effect against a number of oral bacteria. This killing effect requires direct binding of apo-lactoferrin to bacteria and it is not blocked by excess iron. There is evidence that both partly iron-saturated and iron-free forms of lactoferrin may exist simultaneously in human saliva. Recently, it has been demonstrated that within the lactoferrin molecule there are antimicrobial domains (called lactoferricins),

Table 7.2 Major antimicrobial proteins in human whole saliva.

Protein	Major target or function
Non-immunoglobulin proteins	
Lysozyme	Gram-positive bacteria, *Candida* yeasts
Lactoferrin	Gram-positive and –negative bacteria
Peroxidases	Bacteria, viruses, yeasts, decomposition of H_2O_2
Agglutinins	Oral bacteria
Histidine-rich proteins (histatins)	Antibacterial, antifungal
Defensins	Antibacterial, antifungal
Cystatins	Antiviral
Immunoglobulins	
Secretory IgA	Inhibition of adhesion
IgG	Enhancement of phagocytosis
IgM	Enhancement of phagocytosis (?)

which may be released by host or microbial proteases. Furthermore, fragments inhibiting adherence of S. *mutans* to saliva-coated hydroxyapatite have been identified. It is likely that the lactoferricin domains are released also during digestion of lactoferrin in the gastrointestinal tract. This supports the idea that salivary proteins can also be involved in the antimicrobial protection of the upper gastrointestinal tract. Lactoferrin has bacteriostatic, bactericidal, fungicidal, antiviral and anti-inflammatory activity.

Peroxidases

There are two different peroxidase enzymes in whole saliva: salivary peroxidase (sometimes called sialoperoxidase) and myeloperoxidase.[6] The former is secreted by the parotid and submandibular glands; the latter is a leukocyte-derived protein entering the mouth mainly via gingival crevices. In whole saliva the proportion of myeloperoxidase of the total peroxidase activity varies from 30 to 75% depending on the extent of inflamed sites in periodontal and mucosal tissues.[6]

Both enzymes catalyse the oxidation of salivary thiocyanate ions (SCN⁻) by H_2O_2 to the antimicrobial component, hypothiocyanite (OSCN⁻).[7]

$$H_2O_2 + SCN^- \longrightarrow OSCN^- + H_2O$$

At pH <6.0, hypothiocyanous acid (HOSCN) is the main form of the oxidation and it is an even more powerful agent against microorganisms than the ionic form. OSCN⁻/HOSCN is a normal component of human whole saliva and plaque fluid and in predentate individuals it exists already at adult concentrations.

Salivary peroxidases have two major functions: antimicrobial activity by OSCN⁻/HOSCN and protection of host proteins and cells from the toxicity of H_2O_2. Peroxidase systems display antimicrobial activity against a variety of microorganisms, such as mutans streptococci (Fig. 7.4), lactobacilli, yeasts, many anaerobes (periodontal pathogens) and even some viruses (herpes simplex type 1, human immunodeficiency virus).[8–10] Of course, these activities depend on the concentration of OSCN⁻/HOSCN, pH and exposure time. In the human mouth, the antimetabolic activity is likely to be more important than the bactericidal effect since increasing concentrations of hypothiocyanite are known to decrease the acid production by dental plaque after stimulation

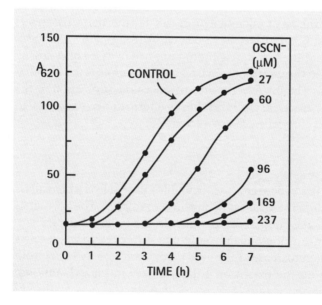

Fig. 7.4 Growth curves of Streptococcus mutans in the presence of increasing concentrations of salivary peroxidase-generated hypothiocyanite (OSCN⁻) ions at pH 6.5. The normal salivary values of hypothiocyanite range from 10 to 50 μM.

by sugars. Interestingly, if SCN^- ions are replaced by I^- ions (or I^- ions are in large excess), the peroxidase-I^--H_2O_2 system is much more powerful against oral and gastrointestinal anaerobes (such as *Helicobacter pylori*) than is hypothiocyanite.[8] Because H_2O_2 is constantly generated in the mouth by aerobic bacteria and H_2O_2 as such is toxic to mucosal and gingival cells,[11] saliva provides peroxidases to consume H_2O_2 by peroxidation. Also, bacterial catalase enzymes can destroy excess H_2O_2.

Other non-immunoglobulin salivary proteins of interest

α-Amylase

α-Amylase is the most abundant salivary enzyme, accounting for approximately 40–50% of the total salivary-gland-produced protein. Amylase mainly (80%) originates from the parotid glands, the rest from the submandibular glands. The biological role of amylase is to split starch into maltose, maltotriose and dextrins. Maltose can be further fermented by oral bacteria to glucose. Salivary amylase clears food debris (containing starch) from the mouth. It also interacts with specific oral bacteria, obviously to some extent modulating their adhesion to pellicles. Swallowed salivary α-amylase is inactivated in the acidic environment of the stomach while pancreatic amylase completes the degradation of starch after the acid gastric juice has been neutralized by the bicarbonate secreted by the pancreas.

Proline-rich proteins and statherin

Human saliva is supersaturated with respect to most calcium phosphate salts but salivary proteins are important in inhibiting spontaneous precipitation of these salts. Such proteins are proline-rich proteins (PRPs) and statherin, which bind calcium and maintain the supersaturated state.

Acidic PRPs comprise as much as 25–30% of all proteins in saliva and they form a complex group with a large number of genetic variants. Some of these inhibit the spontaneous precipitation of calcium phosphate salts, while others adhere to salivary pellicles and selectively promote the adhesion of some bacteria, eg *Streptococcus gordonii* and *Actinomyces viscosus*, to tooth surfaces. PRPs also have the ability to bind tannins, present in such beverages as tea and red wine, and reduce their toxicity.

Statherin, a small protein with only 43 amino acids, originates from both parotid and submandibular glands. The molecule inhibits precipitation of

also some IgM. These antibodies leak into the oral cavity via gingival crevices and also to some extent through the surface of the tongue. Serum antibodies are often specific against oral pathogens, such as mutans streptococci, but no clear-cut evidence of their protective role against dental caries exists either.

Vaccines against dental caries

Three major approaches to develop a vaccine against dental caries have been explored. First, one line of research is focusing on enhancing the common mucosal immune system to produce a high amount of MALT (mucosal-associated lymphoid tissue)-derived sIgA antibodies against mutans streptococci in whole saliva.[13] This enhancement is done by application of high numbers of S. mutans antigens in a short time, intra-orally or –nasally, to stimulate the MALT-system. Also, delivery of antigens in liposomes or co-administered with mucosal adjuvants has been used to enhance the antibody response and related immunological memory. Animal studies have clearly proven some protection against colonization and re-colonization with mutans streptococci as well as some reduction of caries incidence. However, human studies have been only short-term and although effects on bacterial numbers have been observed, no evidence yet exists of a caries preventive effect.

Another approach under active investigation is so-called passive immunization where antibodies are produced outside the body, then enriched and applied to the dentition to protect from mutans streptococci. As 'antibody-fermenters', cow's milk[15] and hen's eggs have proven suitable but also genetic engineering of human-like sIgA antibodies in plants[16] has proven effective. However, no long-term clinical trials of the possible protective effects of these passively administered antibodies have been published. The third approach, now with the most remote possibility of becoming a reality, is the induction of a systemic immune response (IgG) against mutans streptococci (Fig. 7.6). Although successful in monkeys, the potential side-effects of active immunization, such as cross-reactivity of the antigens with heart tissues, makes this approach least tempting.

Effect of ageing on protective functions of saliva

If the flow rate of stimulated saliva remains stable, there is no proof of any decline in the output of salivary sIgA with age. If the person is dentate, the same is true also for IgG and IgM levels in saliva. Thus, the total numbers of antibody molecules do not seem to decline with age. However, the antibody response to

Fig. 7.6 Systemic (s.c.) vaccination by S. mutans has proven quite efficient in animal models but is not considered safe among humans due to possible side-effects of streptococcal antigens.

an antigenic challenge is impaired by age. There is notable evidence that antibody response, eg against mutans streptococci, poliovirus and *Candida albicans*, is weakened after the age of 60–65 years. This might contribute to the rather frequent oral yeast infections among the elderly.

The non-immunoglobulin salivary agents seem to work at full capacity throughout life. Also the functional activity of polymorphonuclear leukocytes in saliva remains stable with age.

Clinical applications of salivary antimicrobial agents

Because of the deepened knowledge of the chemical and functional properties of many host proteins in human saliva, some commercial applications for their use in preventive clinical dentistry have been made.[4] Apart from the short-term vaccination experiments to enhance salivary sIgA (see above), much more interest has been focused on several innate salivary proteins, ie lysozyme, lactoferrin and peroxidases. The idea of their clinical applications seems sound: to add physiological antimicrobial agents into a mouth that lacks saliva-mediated protection (patients with dry mouth), or to enhance saliva's own antimicrobial capacity in infection-prone individuals, such as cancer patients. Many products, comprising one or all of the above components, are already on the market but clinical documentation of their efficacy is rather limited.[4]

There are reports showing a positive response, particularly among patients with xerostomia or cancer treatment but the exact role of the antimicrobial proteins is still unclear. The proteins for these products (toothpastes, mouthrinses, gels, chewing gums) are purified from cow's milk or colostrum because these milk proteins are both structurally and catalytically almost identical to those in human saliva. No adverse effects have reported. Based on a rather long clinical experience, ie over 15 years, these products can be recommended by dentists or physicians to relieve some of the subjective oral symptoms of xerostomia or cancer treatment.

Summary – clinical highlights
An understanding of the multifunctional role of salivary proteins and particularly of their interactions with oral microorganisms is a necessary prerequisite for their clinical applications. This clinical application may include for example, their use in modifying bacterial adhesion to oral surfaces, in eliminating specific pathogens and in designing artificial saliva for patients with dry mouth. A good basic understanding of their mechanisms of action also offers opportunities to combine protective proteins to get the best possible concerted action. This has already been done on a commercial scale.

Assays of individual salivary proteins are of limited or no diagnostic value. This is mainly because they interact in many ways and other proteins often compensate for deficiency in one factor. There is no evidence from a diagnostic point of view that any single salivary protein is more important than the others.

Recently, significant achievements have been made in developing multifunctional, genetically engineered proteins, which carry many of the biological activities described in this chapter. Progress has also been made in the introduction of gene therapy to alleviate salivary gland deficiencies, which tend to become more and more prevalent in ageing populations.

Acknowledgement

I am deeply grateful to Professor William H. Bowen, whose presentations in the previous editions formed the basis for this chapter of this book.

References

1   Tabak L A. In defense of the oral cavity: structure, biosynthesis, and function of salivary mucins. *Ann Rev Physiol* 1995; **57**: 547–564.

2   Tenovuo J. Antimicrobial function of human saliva – how important is it for oral health? *Acta Odontol Scand* 1998; **56**: 250–256.

3   Ericson T, Rundegren J. Characterization of a salivary agglutinin reacting with a serotype c strain of *Streptococcus mutans*. *Eur J Biochem* 1983; **133**: 255–261.

4   Tenovuo J. Clinical applications of antimicrobial host proteins lactoperoxidase, lysozyme and lactoferrin in xerostomia: efficacy and safety. *Oral Diseases* 2002; **8**: 23–29.

5   Lenander-Lumikari M, Månsson-Rahemtulla B, Rahemtulla F. Lysozyme enhances the inhibitory effects of the peroxidase system on glucose metabolism of *Streptococcus mutans*. *J Dent Res* 1992; **71**: 484–490.

6   Thomas E L, Jefferson M M, Joyner R E, Cook G S, King C C. Leukocyte myeloperoxidase and salivary peroxidase: identification and quantitation in human mixed saliva. *J Dent Res* 1994; **73**: 544–555.

7   Thomas E L, Bates K P, Jefferson M M. Hypothiocyanite ion: detection of the antimicrobial agent in human saliva. *J Dent Res* 1980; **59**: 1466–1472.

8. Ihalin R, Loimaranta V, Lenander-Lumikari M, Tenovuo J. The effects of different (pseudo)halide substrates on peroxidase-mediated killing of *Actinobacillus actinomycetemcomitans*. *J Periodont Res* 1998; **33**: 421–427.

9   Välimaa H, Waris M, Hukkanen V, Blankenvoorde M F J, Nieuw Amerongen A V, Tenovuo J. Salivary defense factors in herpes simplex virus infection. *J Dent Res* 2002; **81**: 416–421.

10 Yamaguchi Y, Semmel M, Stanislawski L, Strosberg A D, Stanislawski M. Virucidal effects of glucose oxidase and peroxidase or their protein conjugates on human immunodeficiency virus type 1. *Antimicr Agents Chemother* 1993; **37**: 26–31.

11 Hänström L, Johansson A, Carlsson J. Lactoperoxidase and thiocyanate protect cultured mammalian cells against hydrogen peroxide toxicity. *Medical Biol* 1983; **61**: 268–274.

12 Henskens YMC, Veerman ECI, Nieuw Amerongen AV. Cystatins in health and disease. *Biol Chem Hoppe Seyler* 1996; **377**: 71–86.

13 Childers N K, Tong G, Li F, Dasanayake A P, Kirk K, Michalek S M. Humans immunized with *Streptococcus mutans* antigens by mucosal routes. *J Dent Res* 2002; **81**: 48–52.

14 Kirstilä V, Tenovuo J, Ruuskanen O, Nikoskelainen J, Irjala K, Vilja P. Salivary defense factors and oral health in patients with common variable immunodeficiency. *J Clin Immunol* 1994; **4**: 229–236.

15 Loimaranta V, Tenovuo J, Virtanen S, Marnila P, Syväoja E-L, Tupasela T, Korhonen H. Generation of bovine immune colostrum against *Streptococcus mutans* and *Streptococcus sobrinus* and its effect on glucose uptake and extracellular polysaccharide formation by mutans streptococci. *Vaccine* 1997; **15**: 1261–1268.

16 Ma J K-C, Lehner T, Stabila P, Fux C I, Hiatt A. Assembly of monoclonal antibodies with IgG1 and IgA heavy chain domains in transgenic tobacco plants. *Eur J Immunol* 1994; **24**: 131–138.

Further reading

Bowen W H. Vaccine against dental caries – a personal view. *J Dent Res* 1996; **75**: 1530–1533.

Nieuw Amerongen A V, Veerman E C I. Saliva – the defender of the oral cavity. *Oral Diseases* 2002; **8**: 12–22.

Rudney J. Does variability in salivary protein concentrations influence oral microbial ecology and oral health? *Crit Rev Oral Biol Med* 1995; **6**: 343–367.

Smith D J, Taubman M A. Emergence of immune competence in saliva. *Crit Rev Oral Biol Med* 1993; **4**: 335–341.

Tenovuo J. Oral defense factors in the elderly. *Endod Dent Traumatol* 1992; **8**: 93–98.

Tenovuo J. Salivary parameters of relevance for assessing caries activity in individuals and populations. *Community Dent Oral Epidemiol* 1997; **25**: 82–86.

8

The role of saliva in mineral equilibria – caries, erosion and calculus formation

Bob ten Cate

Introduction

The importance of saliva in the prevention of dental caries is dramatically shown in patients with impaired salivary function. When, as a result of medication or radiation in the oro-facial region, salivary flow is reduced (*see* Chapter 4), the dentition may be completely destroyed within a short period of time. Unlike 'normal' caries, caries as a result of xerostomia is often seen at the incisal or occlusal edges of the teeth and in the cervical region.[1] This can sometimes lead to entire layers of enamel being chipped off even on the smooth surfaces (Figs 8.1, 8.2).

Saliva-pellicle-plaque

Saliva is never in direct contact with the dentition. Even at sites where the plaque is removed by the mechanical cleansing effect of the mucosa or the antagonistic teeth, a thin layer of salivary origin (the 'pellicle') covers the enamel (Fig. 8.3).[2] This layer of salivary proteins and lipids forms immediately after a surface has been completely cleaned, and it has been shown that the pellicle adheres so strongly to the enamel that it is not removed during toothbrushing or prophylaxis. The pellicle protects the enamel to some extent from severe mechanical and chemical damage, the latter for instance imposed by acids in the oral environment.

Laboratory experiments have shown that the pellicle delays the initiation of caries and the dissolution of enamel when teeth are placed in low pH soft drinks.[3] At retention sites the dental plaque forms the second layer separating the tooth surface from saliva. Plaque is mainly composed of bacteria in a polysaccharide matrix. Much attention has recently been given to the liquid phase of plaque (the 'plaque fluid'), as this is the solution often in closest contact with the tooth surface. Mineral dissolution and (re)precipitation processes, as they occur during caries and calculus formation, are directed by the composition of the plaque fluid more than by the composition of saliva, although the two are related (see below).

Enamel composition

The calcified tissues in the body are composed of a calcium phosphate mineral phase and an organic matrix. The latter has different roles, such as forming the 'cement', which holds the mineral crystals together, and regulating their

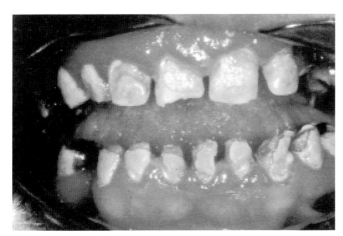

Fig. 8.1 Caries in a patient with impaired salivary function as result of radiation therapy (courtesy of Drs Jansma and Vissink, RUG, the Netherlands).

Fig. 8.2 Electronmicroscopic picture of enamel surface with radiation caries, showing the characteristic chipping of the layers of enamel (courtesy of Drs Jansma and Vissink, RUG, the Netherlands).

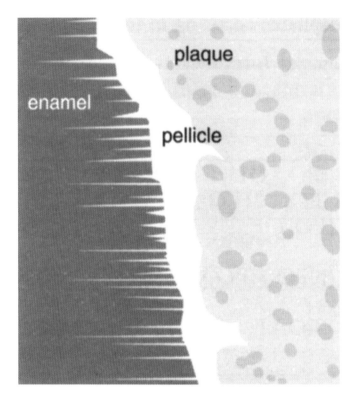

Fig. 8.3 Schematic representation of the interface between enamel and the oral fluids, showing the acquired enamel pellicle and the plaque with bacteria and the plaque matrix.

formation and regeneration. In enamel, the tissue-forming cells (ameloblasts) secrete an organic matrix onto which crystallites are laid down. This is a process which takes place prior to the eruption of the tooth into the oral cavity. Once erupted, the ameloblasts (being on the outside of the tooth) are worn off and the fate of the enamel is no longer determined by cellularly driven mechanisms, but by the interactions between the oral fluids (the term 'oral fluid', in this chapter, refers to saliva and plaque fluid) and the enamel.

In dentine, on the other hand, the odontoblasts, being on the pulpal side, remain active and deposit secondary dentine after eruption, or tertiary dentine as a result of a chemical or mechanical insult to the teeth. This can be seen as a natural defence mechanism of the body against caries and mechanical trauma. For enamel, the body has to rely on saliva as a protective substance.

Saliva contains a number of components that have a specific role in this respect. The above-mentioned organic constituents, proteins and lipids, form

Table 8.1 Calcium phosphates occurring in the body

Mineral	Chemical formula	Calcium concentration at equilibrium at pH = 7, Ca/P = 0.16 and μ = 0.06.
Hydroxyapatite	$Ca_{10}(PO_4)_6(OH)_2$	0.105 mmol/l
Brushite	$CaHPO_4.2H_2O$	0.560 mmol/l
Btricalcium phosphate	$Ca_3(PO_4)_2$	0.165 mmol/l
Octacalcium phosphate	$Ca_8(HPO_4)_2(PO_4)_4.5H_2O$	0.369 mmol/l
Fluorapatite	$Ca_{10}(PO_4)_6F_2$	0.013 mmol/l at [F] = 0.2 ppm
		0.018 mmol/l at [F] = 0.02 ppm

the enamel pellicle which is a diffusion barrier to acids formed in the dental plaque, and in general regulates dissolution and precipitation processes. Of similar importance are the inorganic components, especially calcium and phosphate ions. In its composition saliva possesses features similar to those of the other body fluids, although the degree of saturation to minerals is different.

The mineral phase of enamel consists of an impure hydroxyapatite, HAP (Table 8.1). This mineral is the least soluble in a range of calcium phosphates that are found in nature, and more specifically in the body.[4] Two characteristics of this substance need to be discussed in relation to their importance in the oral environment. Firstly, hydroxyapatite is very permissive in incorporating foreign ions in the crystalline lattice. These may be either positively charged (sodium, potassium, zinc or strontium ions) or negatively charged (fluoride or carbonate ions). The concentrations of these impurities in the tissue are influenced by their presence during its formation. These mineral modifications have either a positive or a negative effect on the solubility: carbonate incorporation makes the apatite more soluble, while fluoride incorporation makes it less soluble.

Secondly, the solubility of the apatite mineral depends highly on the pH of the environment. In an acid environment (low pH), the concentration of ions in the liquid phase surrounding the crystallites necessary to maintain saturation is higher than at high pH. pH is therefore the driving force for dissolution and precipitation of hydroxyapatite. Apart from such physico-chemical considerations, other regulatory mechanisms exist, also in saliva. One example of this is 'nucleators' for precipitation: solutions that are supersaturated with respect to a given mineral do not necessarily precipitate unless this precipitate can form onto a surface. For calculus formation these nucleators are the plaque bacteria, which facilitate mineralization of the plaque. In enamel in contact with saliva or plaque fluid, mineral deposition may occur onto the hydroxyapatite crystallites.

In its most simple form the dissolution and reprecipitation can be described as:

$$Ca_{10}(PO_4)_6(OH)_2 \underset{neutral}{\overset{acid}{\rightleftharpoons}} 10\,Ca^{2+} + 6\,PO_4^{3-} + 2\,OH^-$$

$$+ \qquad +$$
$$6\,H^+ \qquad 2\,H^+$$

$$\updownarrow \qquad \updownarrow$$

$$6\,HPO_4^{2-} \qquad 2\,H_2O$$

Saliva and the Stephan curve

The mineral composition of saliva and plaque fluid is given in Table 8.2. These data show that differences in composition exist between saliva and plaque fluid, even though they are presumed to be in equilibrium. At this stage one can only speculate about the causes of this observation. Possibly the 'solid' phase of the plaque exchanges ions with the plaque fluid very slowly, which, due to its capillary nature, is never in true equilibrium with the saliva. The calcium and phosphate content and in particular the pH of these liquids determine whether enamel will dissolve (leading to caries) and whether mineral may be precipitated (which would result in calculus formation). Figure 8.4 shows the relationship between the saliva and plaque fluid calcium and phosphate levels and the saturation lines for enamel and dentine. It should be noted that the degree of saturation differs between salivas from the various glands and with secretion rate. For instance, saliva is more supersaturated (with respect to HAP and fluorapatite = FAP) at a higher secretion rate.

Table 8.2 Calcium, phosphate and fluoride levels in human stimulated whole saliva and plaque fluid

Saliva:	Approximate concentration ranges			
	mmol/l		ppm	
Calcium	0.75–1.75		30–70	
Phosphate	2.0–5.0		60–155	
Fluoride	0.0005–0.005		0.01–0.10	
Plaque fluid:	**Mean (SD) values**			
	mmol/l		ppm	
Calcium ion	0.85	(0.52)	34	(21)
Phosphate	11.5	(3.3)	356	(102)
Fluoride	0.0049	(0.0027)	0.09	(0.05)

Caries and calculus formation may be explained from Figure 8.4. At physiological pH, saliva and plaque fluid are supersaturated with respect to the hydroxyapatite phase of enamel. This implies that HAP will precipitate if a suitable precipitation nucleus is available. However, after eating foods or drinks containing fermentable carbohydrates, acids are formed in the plaque leading to a fall in pH called a 'Stephan curve' (*see* Fig. 6.1). When the pH is lowered, the concentration of ions needed for saturation increases and in the pH range around 5.6 the tissues will start to dissolve to maintain saturation. The lower the pH, the faster this demineralization. As a result, the phosphate and hydroxyl ions released will take up protons (H^+) thus slowing down or reversing the fall in pH. Consumption of foods or drinks containing fermentable carbohydrates also increases salivary flow; the increased buffering power of saliva, and the washing out of remaining sugars and acids from plaque, contribute to the pH-rising phase of the Stephan curve.

During the recovery phase the plaque gradually becomes saturated and later supersaturated with HAP, and mineral may reprecipitate. Ideally, this occurs at the sites 'damaged' during the demineralization. As mentioned before, the exact

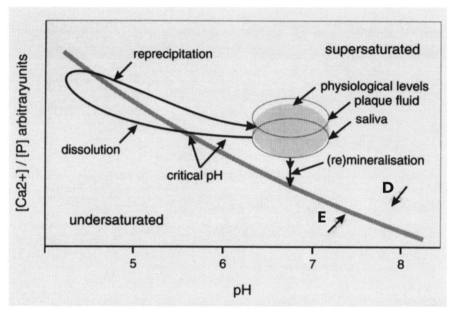

Fig. 8.4 Solubility isotherms (schematic) for enamel (E) and dentine (D) in relation to the levels of calcium and phosphate of saliva and plaque fluid. The change in pH after carbohydrate consumption, and the consequences for saturation of the oral fluids are also indicated.

composition of the apatite formed depends on the composition of the solution from which it is precipitated, in this case the plaque fluid. If, for instance, fluoride is present, this will 'co-precipitate' to form a fluoridated hydroxyapatite. In short, this periodic cycling of pH results in a step-by-step modification of the chemical composition of the outer layers of enamel, becoming somewhat less soluble with time. This process is known as the post-eruptive maturation of the enamel.

It has been argued that some demineralization is beneficial because it will remove the more soluble components of enamel, rich in carbonate, which may be replaced with a fluoride-rich component making the enamel more resistant to subsequent demineralization.

Caries and remineralization

If frequency of carbohydrate consumption is too high, the redeposition of mineral (during the Stephan curve) is far from complete and there is a cumulative

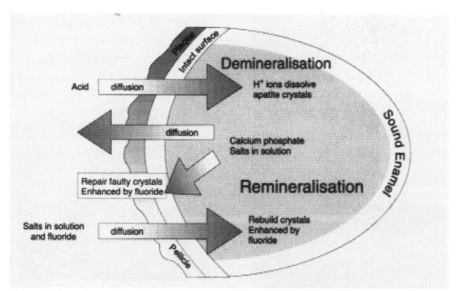

Fig. 8.5 Schematic cross-section of the enamel–pellicle–plaque interface with the diffusion, disolution and precipitation processes occurring during caries development and regression. (Redrawn from reference 7.)

loss of enamel substance. Then a caries lesion will be formed, which is often the 'forerunner' of the caries cavity. A caries lesion is characterized by subsurface loss of mineral while the surface, due to its lower solubility, remains apparently intact. Only small pores are 'etched' in the surface layer at sites corresponding with the interprismatic regions.[5] These enable the transport of acids into the deeper layers of the tissue and of dissolved ions out of the tissue (Fig. 8.5).

Even when a lesion has been formed, saliva can play an important role in preventing excessive decay. With improved oral hygiene or other preventive measures (eg fluoride), deposition of mineral from saliva or plaque fluid may take place instead of further tissue loss. In a laboratory model, remineralization can be illustrated when early enamel lesions are immersed in saliva. From the radiographic pictures (Fig. 8.6) the disappearance of the radiopacities is evident.

Clinically, remineralization was documented in a longitudinal study of drinking water fluoridation[8] and more recently in various toothpaste clinical trials.[7] In the Dutch Tiel Culemborg study the investigators noted that 50% of the lesions seen at the first molar buccal surfaces of 8-year-old children disappeared during the next seven years. Factors put forward to explain this

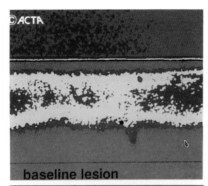

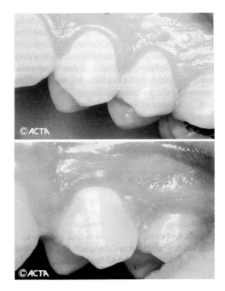

Fig. 8.7 Examples of active (top) and arrested (bottom) lesions.

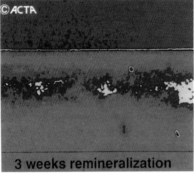

Fig. 8.6 Pseudo coloured radiographs of sections taken from lesions before and after a three-week immersion in saliva, showing the disappearance of the lesion as a result of saliva-induced remineralization.

finding were the further eruption of the teeth, which brought the lesions out of the area at risk and in direct contact with saliva from which the remineralization took place. A closer look at the data revealed that the lesions were seen at rather different stages. In some cases the surfaces appeared chalky and dull, while others were yellowish and shiny. It was concluded that the first type (found more often in the non-fluoridated town) indicated an active caries lesion. The dull appearance was due to recently exposed (non-light reflecting), acid 'treated' enamel, a phenomenon also seen after the deliberate acid etching of enamel prior to placing sealants or composites. The shiny appearance of 'arrested' lesions (found more often in the fluoridated town) was due to the deposition of mineral and organic components from saliva in the porous carious enamel (Fig. 8.7).

With time such lesions will also accumulate dyes from food and, unless completely remineralized, eventually develop into 'brown spots'.

Erosion

Acids formed in dental plaque are the cause of dental caries. Recently, attention has also been given to a different group of acids, those which are present in foods and drinks and which have a direct eroding effect on the dentition.[8] Various reviews report that around 30% of adolescents show signs of erosion in their dentition and that erosion is also often seen in very young patients. In erosion tissue loss does not occur by subsurface demineralization but by a layer-wise removal of enamel or dentine. The pH in such cases is substantially lower than in dental plaque, with values between pH 2 and 3 not being uncommon in beverages. Apart from being caused by so-called extrinsic sources, erosion may result from gastric fluids (at pH below 1) when patients suffer from eating disorders resulting in frequent vomiting or gastroesophageal reflux. Not only is erosion different from caries at the microscopic level, also the distribution around the oral cavity is typical and indicates where acids first come in contact with the dentition and where protective factors are present. The most common site for erosion in some patients is the lingual aspect of mandibular molars. This points to the role of serous saliva and salivary pellicle in protecting the dentition against erosion.[9] Studies to correlate saliva properties with susceptibility to erosion have shown that a low buffer capacity will make individuals more prone to erosion. Salivary flow rates have not been shown to be related to erosion at the individual level. Also in laboratory studies saliva, probably in particular salivary mucins and pellicle, has been shown to slow down the rate of tissue loss.[10] As dental erosion is caused by fluids with very low pH it is easy to explain why fluoride, calcium and phosphate additions have little or no effect in its aetiology. It would require massive amounts of one of these ions to come near to saturation for either HAP or FAP. Recent studies to increase both pH and ion composition have resulted in a beverage with reduced risk for erosion.[11] Obviously such changes to the gastric fluids which cause erosion are not possible.

Calculus

Plaque is supersaturated with respect to many of the calcium phosphate minerals listed in Table 8.1. Mineralization inhibitors present in plaque prevent these minerals from precipitating unless the inhibitors are degraded by enzymes or nucleators for precipitation are present. It has been shown that dead or 'dying' bacteria (or components from bacterial cell walls) serve as nuclei for precipitation. Unlike in enamel, where the calcium phosphate mineral is present as HAP, in calculus four different calcium phosphates may be found, with the distribution of minerals being determined by the age of the deposit.[12]

Because salivary secretions are the main sources of calcium and phosphate in the oral cavity, calculus forms most abundantly on the tooth surfaces opposite the orifices of the main salivary glands. Saliva secretion from the parotid glands may lead to calculus formation on the buccal surfaces of the maxillary molars, while submandibular saliva may contribute to calculus deposition on the lingual surfaces of the mandibular anterior teeth (for more details see Chapter 5). In addition to the difference between calculus at various sites around the mouth, the variation in calculus from supra- and subgingival parts of the tooth should be mentioned. Both are formed as a result of the mineralization of dental plaque, but for subgingival calculus, crevicular fluid and exudate from infected periodontal tissue substitute for saliva in providing the materials from which calculus is formed. Subgingival calculus develops from subgingival plaque, a process that is not necessarily related to a prior formation of supragingival calculus. Chemical analyses have shown that the mineral density of subgingival calculus is higher, which makes it even harder to remove by a dentist or hygienist. The rate at which calculus forms is variable among individuals. In general, supragingival calculus forms first on the lingual aspects of the lower anterior teeth.

Individual variations in plaque fluid and saliva saturation and caries

Variation in the composition of the oral fluids occurs between different sites in the mouth as well as between individuals.[13] The resulting differences in degree of saturation are very small compared with the dramatic changes occurring after acid formation in the plaque. Nevertheless, researchers have for many years been seeking to identify correlations between one individual's caries experience and his/her calcium and phosphate levels or resting pH of saliva and plaque. Recently, techniques have become available for the analysis of very small volumes (nanoliters), which has made plaque fluid the focus of this research. For the latter fluid a difference in degree of supersaturation (with respect to apatite) has been observed between caries-susceptible and caries-free subjects. These data revealed that this difference in supersaturation is primarily caused by a 0.3 unit higher pH value for the plaque fluid of the caries-free individuals.[14] Apparently, although very small, the difference in saturation has clinical implications, presumably by the difference in remineralization potential between the respective plaque fluids. Studies to find indicators for patients at risk for caries have similarly showed that the degree of supersaturation of saliva to fluorapatite showed a high correlation with caries progression. It is argued that in particular fluoride levels in the oral fluids are an important prognostic tool.

Modifying saliva to favour caries prevention and prevent calculus formation

Caries and calculus formation are both caused by dental plaque. The most obvious direct method of their prevention would therefore be effective mechanical plaque removal (eg toothbrushing) or antimicrobial therapy. However, neither has been very effective. It seems that effective plaque removal is almost impossible to achieve by patients.[15] Likewise, antimicrobial approaches in caries prevention have, so far, not been very successful. Prevention therefore relies mainly on changing the physico-chemical mechanisms of caries and calculus, in other words once the bacteria have done their job! In the intrinsic mechanisms of caries prevention saliva has an important part, with its capacity of buffering the acid and clearing the oral cavity of foods or drinks containing fermentable carbohydrates and acids (*see* Chapter 5). Also, saliva affects bacterial growth and metabolism (*see* Chapter 7).

Caries
The presence of fluoride in the oral fluids, derived from topical applications, water, toothpastes, rinses or tablets, has a significant depressing effect on the initiation and progression of dental caries, as shown in many epidemiological and clinical studies. The smooth and interproximal surfaces benefit the most from fluoride as a caries preventive agent. During any kind of fluoride usage, fluoride is deposited at retention sites in the oral cavity. These can be porous regions (such as caries lesions) in the dentition or the soft tissues. Fluoride,

when given in sufficiently large concentrations, may also be laid down on the teeth as globular calcium fluoride deposits.[16] While in aqueous solutions pure calcium fluoride is very soluble, in the oral cavity it is surprisingly stable. This is thought to be due to the presence of a protective outer layer on the globules, formed by a reaction between calcium fluoride and phosphate and proteins from saliva. These globules may act as fluoride slow-release devices.

Saliva also serves as a carrier for fluoride-ions from the various depots to the sites at risk for caries in the oral cavity. In clinical studies on the effects of fluoride dentifrices it was observed that the depot formation resulted in an elevation of the fluoride levels in plaque and saliva throughout the day.[6] After cessation of the use of fluoride dentifrices it took about two weeks for the fluoride in plaque and saliva to return to 'baseline' levels. Now more attention is given to the patient's usage of toothpaste, which apart from brushing methods and frequency, considers what should be done after toothbrushing to guarantee optimal retention of the fluoride in the oral cavity. One advice given is to minimize the amount of water to rinse out the mouth, or to use the dentifrice (tap water diluted) as a mouthrinse.[18] Even low fluoride levels in plaque or saliva are effective in caries inhibition, because they inhibit the demineralization of enamel and enhance the remineralization, by an increased rate of mineral deposition. Equally important to note is that this deposition then occurs as a fluoridated apatite, which is less susceptible to demineralization during subsequent acid challenges. The success of fluoride has initiated studies to increase the salivary levels of other 'common' ions of apatite, calcium and phosphate or the pH. Phosphate, amongst others as food additive, has been widely studied, but was never found to be very beneficial in humans.

Many currently available toothpastes contain calcium, which is reported to have an additional preventive effect. Also xylitol is now added to chewing gum and to some dentifrices (*see* Chapter 6). The working mechanism relies in particular on the xylitol-enhanced salivary flow and on its antibacterial properties. The clinical effects of each of these xylitol additions are yet to be established or confirmed. Another ingredient added to dentifrices aimed at supporting saliva in its caries preventive action is bicarbonate. Bicarbonate addition increases the pH of the oral fluids, which, in conjunction with fluoride, enhances mineral deposition.

Root surface caries

Caries of the root surface has received increasing attention due to the longevity of the teeth.[19] As a result of medication and of diseases or surgery of the periodontal tissues, the root surface often becomes exposed to the oral cavity when the patient gets older. The tissues of the root surface are particularly vulnerable to acid attacks and subsequently to proteolytic breakdown of the collagen matrix. Fluoride treatments have been shown to prevent this type of caries. When root lesions have formed it is now advised to improve first the local oral hygiene and give fluoride applications. This leads to a saliva-induced rehardening of the dentine; restorative treatment can follow if indicated.

Calculus

Agents contained in dentifrices are now available which interfere with calculus formation. Crystal growth inhibitors (such as pyrophosphate and zinc citrate) are very effective in reducing the amounts of supragingival calculus, while the calculus that does form can be more easily removed.

Saliva stimulation

Stimulated saliva contains higher levels of bicarbonate buffer and is more supersaturated with respect to hydroxyapatite than unstimulated saliva. If, after sugar intake, saliva stimulation is prolonged (eg by chewing sugar-free gum) two beneficial effects may follow: the increased bicarbonate prevents the pH of plaque from falling and thus reduces the potential for hydroxyapatite dissolution, and the increased saturation raises the potential for remineralization of any damaged crystallites (*see also* Chapter 6). These effects have been demonstrated experimentally using pieces of enamel from extracted teeth attached to the dentitions of volunteers, and have been confirmed in clinical trials.

Concluding remarks

As outlined above, components from saliva interact in different ways with the dentition in attempts to protect the teeth from becoming carious or from excessive calculus formation. In addition, saliva is the oral transport medium by which preventive agents are distributed around the mouth. Patients who lack sufficient saliva suffer from many oral diseases, of which caries is only one. To alleviate the discomfort, they are advised to use saliva stimulants and substitutes which have the function of lubricating the oral surfaces. Most substitutes are developed for their rheological and wetting properties, more than for their chemical composition (buffer capacity, calcium, phosphate, fluoride). It is recommended therefore that these products should be better formulated for their potential to mimic natural saliva also in its caries preventive properties.

Clinical highlights

- The arrest and/or reversal of early caries lesions is a natural and very important means of caries prevention which can be enhanced by intervention.

- Saliva contains calcium and phosphate in a state supersaturated with respect to hydroxyapatite. As a result, saliva reduces the dissolution of tooth mineral in caries, and replaces mineral (that is, remineralizes the crystals) in early lesions. Salivary hypofunction will eliminate both these functions. Salivary stimulation increases its potential for remineralization.

- Fluoride in the mouth inhibits demineralization if it is present in the aqueous phase between the enamel crystals at the time of an acid challenge.

- Fluoride enhances remineralization of early lesions by helping calcium and phosphate, derived primarily from saliva, to regrow the surfaces of partially dissolved crystals. This will produce a fluorapatite-like surface, which is more resistant to subsequent acid attack. Hence strategies which maintain the ambient level of fluoride in saliva can help control caries.

- From a clinical viewpoint, a continual supply of elevated levels of fluoride in the mouth is a very effective preventive measure against caries.

- Methods which deliver fluoride to the mouth (water, toothpaste, mouthrinses or professionally applied topicals) are very effective in caries prevention, even in patients with severely reduced salivary flow. In fact, fluoride is essential in these patients.

- Because of the supersaturation of saliva, calculus formation would occur much more generally were there no inhibitors of calcification present in saliva and plaque.

- Teeth in direct contact with strong acids (food or gastric) will be eroded. This process is somewhat delayed by saliva-derived pellicle or salivary mucins.

References

1   Vissink A, Burlage F R, Spijkervet F K, Jansma J, Coppes R P. Prevention and treatment of the consequences of head and neck radiotherapy. *Crit Rev Oral Biol Med* 2003; **14**: 213–25.

2   Hannig M. Ultrastructural investigation of pellicle morphogenesis at two different intraoral sites during a 24-h period. *Clin Oral Investig* 1999; **3**: 88–95.

3   Hannig M, Balz M. Influence of in vivo formed salivary pellicle on enamel erosion. *Caries Res* 1999; **33**: 372–9.

4   Posner A S, Beebe R A. The surface chemistry of bone mineral and related calcium phosphates. *Semin Arthritis Rheum* 1975; **4**: 267–91.

5   Arends J, Christoffersen J, Christoffersen M R, Ogaard B, Dijkman A G, Jongebloed W L. Rate and mechanism of enamel demineralization in situ. *Caries Res* 1992; **26**: 18–21.

6   Groeneveld A. Longitudinal study of prevalence of enamel lesions in a fluoridated and non-fluoridated area. *Community Dent Oral Epidemiol* 1985; **13**: 159–63.

7   Biesbrock A R, Faller R V, Bartizek R D, Court L K, McClanahan S F. Reversal of incipient and radiographic caries through the use of sodium and stannous fluoride dentifrices in a clinical trial. *J Clin Dent* 1998; **9**: 5–10.

8   ten Cate J M, Imfeld T. Dental erosion, summary. *Eur J Oral Sci* 1996; **104**: 241–4.

9   Young W G, Khan F. Sites of dental erosion are saliva-dependent. *J Oral Rehabil* 2002; **29**: 35–43.

10   Meurman J H, Frank R M. Scanning electron microscopic study of the effect of salivary pellicle on enamel erosion. *Caries Res* 1991; **25**: 1–6.

11   West N X, Hughes J A, Parker D M, Moohan M, Addy M. Development of low erosive carbonated fruit drinks 2. Evaluation of an experimental carbonated blackcurrant drink compared to a conventional carbonated drink. *J Dent* 2003; **31**: 361–5.

12   White D J. Recent advances in methods for the assessment of dental calculus—research and clinical implications. *Monogr Oral Sci* 2000; **17**: 163–73.

13   Tenovuo J. Salivary parameters of relevance for assessing caries activity in individuals and populations. *Community Dent Oral Epidemiol* 1997; **25**: 82–6.

14   Margolis H C, Duckworth J H, Moreno E C. Composition and buffer capacity of pooled starved plaque fluid from caries-free and caries-susceptible individuals. *J Dent Res* 1988; **67**: 1476–82.

15   Bellini H T, Arneberg P, von der Fehr F R. Oral hygiene and caries. A review. *Acta Odontol Scand* 1981; **39**: 257–65.

16   Petzold M. The influence of different fluoride compounds and treatment conditions on dental enamel: a descriptive in vitro study of the CaF_2 precipitation and microstructure. *Caries Res* 2001; **35**(Suppl. 1): 45–51.

17   Duckworth R M, Morgan S N. Oral fluoride retention after use of fluoride dentifrices. *Caries Res* 1991; **25**: 123–9.

18   Sjogren K, Birkhed D, Rangmar S, Reinhold A C. Fluoride in the interdental area after two different post-brushing water rinsing procedures. *Caries Res* 1996; **30**: 194–9.

19   Anusavice K J. Dental caries: risk assessment and treatment solutions for an elderly population. *Compend Contin Educ Dent* 2002; **23**: 12–20.

Further reading

Featherstone J D B. Diffusion phenomena and enamel caries development. In Guggenheim B (Ed) *Cariology Today*. International Congress, Zurich, 1983. Basel: S Karger, 1984; 259–68.

Mandel I D. Calculus formation and prevention: An overview. *Compend Contin Educ Dent Suppl* 1987; **8**: 235–241.

Ten Cate J M. The effect of fluoride on enamel de- and remineralisation in vitro and in vivo. In Guggenheim B (Ed) Cariology Today International Congress, Zurich, 1983, Basel: S Karger, 1984; 231–6.

Nauntofte B, Tenovuo J O, Lagerlöf F. Secretion and composition of saliva. In Fejerskov O, Kidd E (Eds) *Dental Caries The Disease and its Clinical Management.* pp 7–28. Oxford: Blackwell Munksgaard, 2003.

Index